"In a time w[...] so thankful that the Lord has anointed people to restore and heal broken relationships. Dr. Donald Frazier offers valuable insights in this book that can not only heal a marriage but also totally transform lives. In *The Prodigal Spouse*, he offers practical advice and solid biblical counsel—to those who have already walked through marital failure as well as to those who want to avoid it. "

J. Lee Grady, Editor
Charisma Magazine

"I highly recommend Donald Frazier's *The Prodigal Spouse* not only for its very helpful insights on marriage, but also for the refreshing originality in the scriptural framework for its presentation. This book will be a valuable resource for pastors, counselors, and couples who need to hear its message."

Dr. Vinson Synan
Regent University/School of Divinity

"Just like the prodigal son, you may be lost, but you can find your way back. In *The Prodigal Spouse*, Dr. Frazier examines in infinite detail how quickly one can fall into the sinful state of adultery. He also examines how this sinful fall can be avoided. Straightforward, no-nonsense biblical instruction is offered to those who become separated from God's will. Whether you are the adulterer or the betrayed, you will find encouragement and direction on how to return to God. Don't wait until you're confronted with failure, ruin, and despair; find out how to avoid the trappings of the world and of the flesh—find out how to overcome."

Marcus D. Lamb
President & CEO, Daystar Television

"Infidelity rips the heart out of any relationship. In *The Prodigal Spouse* Dr. Frazier presents a clear, concise understanding of the path to Brokenness and restoration. A wonderful tool for couples and counselors."

Dr. Tim Clinton, President
American Association of Christian Counselors

the
prodigal
spouse

the
prodigal
spouse

The trials, the tears, and the trail for heading
home and healing a broken marriage

Dr. Donald M. Frazier

TATE PUBLISHING & *Enterprises*

Published by Tate Publishing & Enterprises, LLC
127 E. Trade Center Terrace | Mustang, Oklahoma 73064 USA
1.888.361.9473 | www.tatepublishing.com

Tate Publishing is committed to excellence in the publishing industry. The company reflects the philosophy established by the founders, based on Psalm 68:11,
"The Lord gave the word and great was the company of those who published it."

Book design copyright © 2008 by Tate Publishing, LLC. All rights reserved.
Cover design by Leah LeFlore
Interior design by Joey Garrett

Published in the United States of America

ISBN: 978-1-60604-231-1
1. Christian Living: Relationships
2. Church & Ministry: Ministry Resources: Family Ministry/Pastoral Helps: Pastoral Care & Counseling
08.05.06

This book is dedicated to the many individuals and couples who have entrusted me with the accounts of their pain and anguish resulting from marital infidelity. You opened your hearts to me, your counselor, as you sought my guidance and support. Your stories have made this book possible.

While I share the collective essence of your personal tragedies, I have not divulged any of your personal information. I have consistently held your confidence inviolate. That is a trust I shall never breach.

acknowledgments

There are three elements to our lives that have profound impact upon us. The first is called "Blessings." These are the daily physical and spiritual provisions that we receive from our Heavenly Father. Blessings may be tangible or intangible, but they are, nonetheless, critical for the ongoing function of our earthly existence. Psalms 68:19 says, "Blessed *be* the Lord, *who* daily loadeth us *with benefits, even* the God of our salvation."

The second element is called "Assets." These represent the accumulation of blessings that has exceeded our basic upkeep. We see them in the form of homes, furnishings, jewelry, vehicles, boats, planes, bank accounts, retirement funds, and various other material goods. Many people live their lives with the goal of accumulating as many assets as they possibly can. To the greedy go the spoils!

The third element in our lives is called "Treasures." Now this category can be completely subjective. We have all heard the slogan "One man's trash is another man's treasure." That proves that not only beauty but also value is in the eye of the beholder. Treasures are the things that we consider priceless.

For me, I continue daily to count my blessings that God has lavished upon me. However, being a minister for all of my adult life has not lent itself to being able to accumulate a significant portfolio of assets that would impress Wall Street. My wife, Abbie, and I enjoy our modest home with a mortgage, two cars, our eclectic furniture most of which was either given to us or purchased at resale shops or yard sales, and *the* checking account through which passes whatever income we receive. Nevertheless, by all accounts, we are blessed. While I do not have an impressive inventory of assets, I have an enormous collection of treasures.

What makes my treasures so priceless to me is that they share one common denominator: they all walk upright. My treasures are the *people* who have enriched my life. They are the family God gave me and the friends I have been blessed with along the way. At the end of the day, it is the people in our lives that truly enrich us. Assets can be affected by a volatile financial market, but family and friends will be there when the assets are long gone.

My treasure chest begins with my immediate family, which originated with my two parents, Roy and Elizabeth, who, though departed from this life, still impact me daily with the exemplary lives they lived for Christ. Then, my two brothers, Roy, Jr. and Micheal, who, along with their families, have endeared themselves to me. My life would be less than complete without them.

The largest portion of my treasure chest is occupied by my precious wife, Abbie. Since 1970, we have managed to pursue our dream: two imperfect people trying to make a perfect marriage. We are not there yet, but we have come a long way, and we are closer now to that dream than we have ever been.

From our humble beginnings as a couple, we have been

enriched by the arrival of our two sons, Jeremy Prentice and Jason Matthew. They have brought enormous joy, laughter, and parental pride to us. I am thankful to them for sparing us many of the sorrows and calamities that youthful ignorance and carelessness brought to other families. They made parenting easy for us, and that was a blessing since Abbie and I were rookies at the task. Thank God, we all survived the experience and are still on "hugging terms" with each other.

Our family takes great comfort in the wonderful assurance provided by our loving Lord for our babies who could not be carried full-term. Of our six pregnancies, only our two sons, Jeremy and Jason, survived the full nine months. We have four precious little sons or daughters, and Jeremy and Jason have four siblings, awaiting us when we arrive "home." We do not have them now, but we will enjoy them for eternity. In heaven, our family circle will forever be *unbroken*. One of our first joys of heaven will be when we see these four beautiful faces and hear them tell us their names … the ones God gave them when He wrote them in the Book of Life from the foundation of the world (Revelation 17:8).

My treasure chest expanded with the arrival of Jason's wife, Regina Leigh. This beautiful and precious young lady has become a vibrant woman of God, serving beside Jason in his ministerial calling. She and Jason have given us three grandchildren who, we believe, are perfect in every way. Mackenzie, who along with her brothers, Micah and Joshua, brings out a love we never knew until we had "The Adorables" join our family. Grandparenting is the time to *get right* what you *got wrong* the first time around.

Jeremy, though older than Jason, did not marry until later. He brought into our family three treasures: Rebecca Leigh became his wife, and she is an outstanding woman of strength, combined with enormous compassion. Becky has a sense of humor that was born to be a part of our family; she also brought her twins, Kyra and Quint, and they are adorable indeed. We loved each of them from the moment we met them. Their support has helped make this book a reality.

I could not possibly mention everyone who is a treasure to me. I do want to cite several friends who have made a lasting impact upon me with their friendships. I am deeply indebted to Gil and Dr. DeEtte Morgan. They have been friends and partners in our ministry for over thirty years. Gil served on our Board of Directors when we incorporated our ministry. He is a Certified Public Accountant who has meticulously and faithfully donated his services to us as we sought to serve our Lord in ministry. They are incalculable treasures in my life.

The treasure chest also includes my music mentor, Dr. C. Otis Forrest. Otis is by all accounts a musical genius, yet with the heart of a servant. He has assisted my ministry for over forty years in numerous ways with tutoring, producing, and recording my music. Otis has always been a friend when I needed a friend to lean upon. He is a treasure whose value is priceless.

The value of treasure is not measured in how long you have held it. It is not just determined by the supply and demand of the marketplace. The value of your treasure is determined by the significance that it holds in *your* life. Thus entered into my life just a few short years ago a treasure named Dr. Lonnie R. Rex. He is a man of regal renown in the world of religion and humanitarian efforts. I can never be his peer. I cannot begin to rise to the level of this man's accomplishments for the world and the Kingdom of God.

Dr. Rex, who has dined with kings and queens, been knighted by the Russian government, picnicked with Pope John Paul II prior to having private devotions with him in his personal chapel in the hills outside of Rome, and met with both American and foreign presidents, has become one of my dearest and trusted friends. This book might never have materialized without the supportive efforts of this giant among men. God brought him into my life when I desperately needed *someone* who knew *somebody* who would help a *nobody* get his foot in the door of publishing.

Sir Lonnie R. Rex has exemplified the Scripture, "Don't try to act important but associate yourself with ordinary people" (Romans 12:16, TLB). His friendship is a treasure of inestimable value.

The last treasure I will mention is the indeterminable number of teachers, ministers, professors, and writers who have impacted my educational life. To acknowledge them all would be an utter impossibility. I do wish to refer once again to my "elder brother and brother Elder," Dr. Roy Frazier, a fellow minister with a PhD in Clinical Psychology, whose inspiration and encouragement have been uniquely significant to me in my educational and professional pursuits.

I readily acknowledge that no matter how many names I list as references and influences, I have overlooked some contributors who have added to my storehouse of biblical and behavioral knowledge. I am extremely grateful to all of my ministerial and professional predecessors who have shared the wealth from their intellectual treasury with me. May God bless them throughout eternity for their contributions to society, our marriages, and the Kingdom of our Lord and Savior Jesus Christ.

My late father, The Reverend Roy W. Frazier, used to frequently say, "I milk a lot of cows, but I churn my own butter." That was his way of addressing the *eclecticism* of his ministerial content. He was stating that he read and studied from many sources, but then he homogenized the information into something that had his touch of genius or original-ity. I will "cop the same plea" in this book, except where I quote a source directly.

The remainder of the material will be a paraphrastic of the data, presented in a form for dissemination that I hope you find understandable and informative. These paraphrases are actually verbal vignettes designed to imprint permanently the powerful insights about marriage on your mind.

The majority of my information is based upon a lifetime of study ("milking the cows") followed by the admixture of this knowledge into a personal application that I eagerly share with you, the reader. There is no intent to plagiarize anyone else's work, and every effort has been made to avoid such lapses of integrity. Obviously, I do not claim originality on everything written in this book. I am simply serving you some of my home-churned *butter*. I pray you will be blessed by this integration of the scientific study of relationships with God's inerrant Word.

commendatory

As a reader and examiner of manuscripts for the book-publishing business of the world, I had the book of the Reverend D. M. Frazier, Ph.D., on the *"The Prodigal Spouse"* put into my hands for reading and criticism, that I might report on its character and merits as would either condemn or commend it as a prospective book in the world of literature.

After careful reading and searching criticism, I am induced to make the following report on the same: I find it a manuscript of high literary character … a treasury of scholastic research and merit; an orthodox exposition of divine truth; a historic narration of the Kingdom of God on the earth; a full presentation of God's revelation of Himself to man in His word and in Christ Jesus by the Holy Spirit; a complete discovery of *"The Prodigal Spouse"* as revealed in the Bible; and an exhibition of the Church of God as the light of the world, so that "out of Zion, the perfection of Beauty" God may shine on the darkness of this world to illuminate it.

In every part and characteristic, Dr. Frazier has given a complete work of the subject in hand. It is one of the finest, if not the finest manuscript of high character and substantial merit I have examined. It ought to have a place in the world of books not only, but an immortality in the world's literature.

The Right Reverend S.R. Sanchez,
Doctor of Sacred Theology, St. Thomas-a-Becket
Theological Institute, Canterbury, England
Resident Bishop and Primate of North America
and dependencies of the North American Conference
of the Methodist Church, Wesley Synod

table of contents

introduction

You may be one who is presently married or someone contemplating marriage. If you fit into the latter category, I want to set the stage for you by sharing a pearl of wisdom passed down through the ages that will prepare you for the matrimonial phase of your life. You need to know that after you have gone through the arduous process of finding your soulmate, the one you want to spend the rest of your life with, you will finally stand before the minister and the two of you will get to say, "I do."

When all the plans and preparations are behind you and that glorious moment arrives, when the minister pronounces you "man and wife," you and your spouse will finally be at the end of your troubles. The problem is, you are at the *front* end! Welcome aboard the love boat. There will surely be some choppy waters ahead. Just keep reading, and you will see how to prepare for the storms you will incur.

I am not telling you this because I am a marriage expert, but because I am a marriage survivor. The only experts in this field are those who have never been married. No couple is exempt from difficulties. Our goal is to survive the relationship problems and "inch toward oneness" a step at a time.

Life is a voyage, but it is *not* a vacation. Psychologists use the term "vicissitudes" to describe the ups and downs, peaks and valleys, highs and lows of our "post-mordial" existence here on earth. There is probably no greater area of life where these vicissitudes are manifested than in marriage.

It has become a common mantra of marriage to say that opposites attract. After all, that's what "hetero" means, as in *heterosexual* or *heterodoxy*. The literal translation of that last word means "having a differing or opposite opinion." Yes, you are married to someone with opinions that, for the most part, are going to be very *opposite* of yours. The actual Greek word "hetero" means "another of a different kind" in contrast to "allo" meaning "another of the same kind."

You will never know just how different your spouse is until after you have "tied the knot." You may think those little idiosyncrasies are cute now and that they contributed to your betrothed seeming so special to you before the marriage. Your perspective just might be in for a rude awakening as you hear how opposite those opinions are.

Now you may have already realized that your spouse is not you, doesn't think like you, doesn't act like you, doesn't respond like you, doesn't feel what you feel, and usually thinks *you* are the one who needs fixing. Many couples eventually come to this awareness that opposite really means "opposite," like in North Pole/South Pole opposite. Let me establish a thread of truth that you will see woven throughout this book. Sometimes it will be spoken; at other times it will simply be implied. Here it is in emphatic print so you will not miss it: *Opposites frequently attract. Opposites almost always annoy!*

Medical science tells us that men and women do not think alike. That is a "eureka!" moment that most of you have already discovered just by observation. The data from that discovery tells us that women are more inclined to use the right hemisphere of their brains while men are typically more left-side dominant. A refresher course in cerebral science from Dr. William Betcher's book *Seven Basic Quarrels in Marriage* will remind you that "the left-brain person is more inclined toward science, mathematics, logic, engineering, spatial tasks, architecture, doing/making, aggression/strength, thinking, autonomy and independence." Therefore, this person would be more *concrete* in their thinking and responses.

The right-brain-oriented individual, Betcher suggests, "is more prone toward love, emotions, art, language learning, oral expression, giving/enabling, receptivity/vulnerability, interdependence and connection." Therefore, this person would be more *abstract* in their cognitive processes. There is no "right or wrong" in these assessments. It is just a matter of whether one's dominant cerebral side is "left or right."

As you know, generalizations always have exceptions, and this principle of left-brain/right-brain orientation is no different. There are men who excel at fashion, art, and other areas thought to be more female dominated. Conversely, you will find women who have excelled at left-brain activities such as mathematics, medicine, flying jets, or being commander of an orbiting space shuttle.

What is responsible for these annoyances that are bursting the bubble of our marital bliss? Can we place the blame on something as simple as a power struggle between the cerebral hemispheres? The answer is not "what" but "who" is responsible. In this union of marriage, you have two people. During courtship, a myopic condition prevails that precludes us from seeing what we do not want to see. We keep our vision short ranged and process the dynamics of our betrothed's attitudes and behavior through the grid of "unconditional love." In the context of an engaged couple, that means "to love is to *overlook*."

It is easy to overlook some red flags when you are simmering in the flames of physical attraction. Many couples have naively believed that those red flags would somehow disappear after marriage. Some have been so deluded as to convince themselves that the red flags were never actually there. They chalk it up as pre-wedding jitters or an approach-avoidance complex toward marriage.

If the red flags are there, what do you do about them? The unsuspecting couple can be fearful that they will sabotage the relationship if they address certain behavioral issues before marriage. Obviously, pre-marital counseling with a competent clinician or minister could provide excellent guidance when needing to broach specific areas of concern between the couple. Unfortunately, most couples erroneously believe that everything will become magically better after marriage. That borders on delusional thinking. Obnoxious behaviors or right-brain/left-brain conflicts do not become more attractive because of a marriage license.

Fear of failure and fear of rejection are two major reasons why couples do not confront their pre-wedding concerns. As one noted speaker said, "You will never *change* what you refuse to *confront*." When you discover that your espoused is your "polar opposite," you must make some difficult decisions. If these issues are non-negotiable, the sooner you deal with them, the better. Confrontation may be painful, but it can also be highly productive when done in a caring and loving context.

In the realm of Christian counseling, there is a discipline referred to as "nouthetic counseling." It derives its name from the Greek word *nouthesia*, meaning "to put in mind, to admonish, instruct or to warn." It carries the implication of "training by word." This is in stark contrast to the procedure of "training by act" (*paideia*) or intervention.

Nouthetic counseling therefore incorporates the procedural goal of "change through confrontation, with concern." This expression provides the parameters for personal change. Its goal is to help someone make an informed decision to change his or her behavior and the atmosphere of confrontation is one of concern.

Warnings are daily given out of concern for the safety and welfare of those we love. They may range from "Don't eat the snow" to "Be careful of the speed-trap in this town." We warn because we care!

This counseling discipline allows a format for sharing concerns that impact the marriage. When one of the spouses understands the motivation for being confronted about change is emanating from their partner's heart of love and concern, they usually become less resistant to the process and can see the value of adjusting their behavior to help their spouse. Therefore, in nouthetic counseling the sessions are not all about *me*; they are structured to be all about *us*.

One of the keys to understanding marriage is to agree that, in this new union, you both must give up the luxury of independent living. Neither person can act unilaterally without creating some very serious problems in the relationship. There must be a willingness to discuss and even *compromise* on certain issues. There will be some issues where you will need to *stand your ground*, and, on certain issues, you may need to be totally *deferring* to your spouse. Only the specific couple can know into which category their concerns fall and what the proper course of action should be for the mutual benefit of the parties in the marriage.

Do not forget the earlier statement, "Opposites attract/opposites annoy," because it will help you comprehend more about the dynamics of marriage than just about anything else I will say in this book. Do you remember the reference to those little *idiosyncrasies* or peculiarities we mentioned earlier? Well, after marriage, they can start getting on your last nerve.

Those eccentricities can become just strange, bizarre, abnormal behaviors in your view. They can cease to be attractive and can easily become downright annoying. This insight is important so that you can understand how things can begin a downward spiral of unraveling from what promised to be an idyllic marriage between two loving individuals. You may feel sure your spouse has *morphed* into a person you no longer recognize or find appealing.

You may reach the point in your marriage where you see your spouse as no longer independent, but *stubborn*. They are no longer thrifty, they're *stingy*; no longer laid back, they're just *lazy*; no longer ambitious, they're a *workaholic*; they are no longer decisive, they are *controlling*; no longer mysterious, they're *deceptive*; no longer absentminded, they're *irresponsible*; no longer tidy, they're *obsessive-compulsive;* no longer playful, they're *abusive*; no longer prudish, they're *frigid*; they are no longer uninhibited, they're just plain *perverted*.

Upon candid reflection, you may discover that your spouse really hasn't changed all that much. It is *your perception* of them that has changed so radically. What once made them seem unique now makes them seem *weird*. If you are honest with yourself, you can admit that your spouse has not become a *Dr. Jekyll and Mr. Hyde* since the wedding day. They may have been "Mr. Hyde" all the time; you just didn't want to see it. Everything that annoys you now was there for the viewing during your courtship. You, like most lovers, refused to take off the rose-colored glasses and *really see* what was there to see. Now, the circumstances may have arisen in your marriage where dealing with your "opposite" has really become an annoying and challenging task that seems to be driving the two of you apart!

Marriage continues to be the bedrock for any surviving society. It is the oldest institution in recorded civilization. However, be advised: it is an *institution*! While marriage should differ from other institutions, like penal and mental, it is, nevertheless, an institution. This one can feature the dynamics of a doctor/patient, teacher/pupil, or a warden/inmate relationship or anything in between. A marriage can run the emotional and physical gamut from Disneyland to Alcatraz. It all depends on the participants. Walls are walls! What goes on inside those walls determines whether it is a playhouse or a prison.

Where would comedians be without the subject of marriage as a time-tested source for their humor? Most of their audiences appear to be able to relate easily to a joke about marriage. The humor often resembles something with which they are all too familiar. It could be about the frigid wife, the lazy husband, the honeymoon or honey do's, "the time of the month" or "the time of your life."

Laughter always seems to provide a more appropriate emotional outlet than crying when you delve into the inner sanctum of marriage. At least laughter carries the medicinal value of being good for the endocrine system, which promotes a stronger immunity against certain diseases. For many, laughter is a viable way of coping with their connubial conflicts and thereby extending their marriage misery well into old age.

This book, however, is not about jokes or laughter. This book is about a marital crisis that will usually elicit copious tears of pain and anguish. It is about infidelity. You may rest assured that to the victim, adultery is no laughing matter. Historical, cultural, social, ethnic, economic, educational, and geographical differences between marital partners represent matters requiring adjustments or compromise. These bumps in the road are not uncommon for the average couple.

Infidelity is certainly not just a bump in the road. It is a train wreck. It is a crisis of epic proportion, requiring that your home become an Intensive Care Unit for the wounded. Be assured, there will be casualties. There could even be deaths. It is possible that the marriage will not survive. The outcome will be determined by the course of action taken when such a calamity occurs. This book is written to help you get back on the proper path and, hopefully, to complete your marital journey. You do not have to die emotionally or physically from the horrific tragedy you have experienced. Whether you are the *offender* or the *offended*, there is hope for your recovery.

The Prodigal Spouse is written as a guideline to reveal the seventeen biblical stages of the restoration process as found in Luke 15. They will show you how you can use them to recover from the anguish of adultery. This is not about offering you a Band-Aid to help you cope. You need to conquer this derailment in your marriage. You must conquer!

The word "prodigal" is not found in the KJV Bible but is a practical and commonly used definition of the word "riotous" (verse 13). Because of the richness of its definition, it is perhaps the best word to describe the one committing adultery. The original Greek word is the combination of two words with a literal meaning of "unsavedness." From the consultation of seven Greek and English dictionaries, it also carries the sense of "wasteful, debauched, profligate, excess, indiscriminate lavishness or being dissolute, given to extravagant expenditure, expending money or other things without necessity, recklessly or viciously profuse, not frugal or economical, rashly or wastefully extravagant, unrestrained by convention or morality, squandering deplorably, dissipated and degraded, a person who spends or has spent his or her money or substance with wasteful extravagance, spendthrift, one who is given to wasteful luxury or extravagance."

This process of recovery from infidelity will take time, so please do not get in a hurry. It usually requires a minimum of six months to two years to return to something approximating "normal" after infidelity. For some, the task has taken up to ten years. Recovery time depends on the circumstances of the offense and the parties involved. Some things will expedite healing, and other things will impede the recovery.

One of the factors that impacts the recovery time from adultery is whether the offender is the husband or the wife. There are very different sets of emotional and psychological dynamics that are evident in the two genders when an infidelity occurs. A man can more easily excuse his own infidelity because he usually, though incorrectly, sees it as simply the inevitable result of being physically stimulated by another woman.

Men often say that the other woman did not mean anything to them. It was "just sex" that happened between two consenting adults. The carnal man does not restrict his amorous feelings for just "*the* other woman" but can often find sexual stimulation and temptation from almost *any* other woman. Statistics always verify that, as a group, straying husbands have more sexual partners than straying wives. With this masculine view, an unfaithful husband will seldom apply himself to the restoration process as diligently as will an unfaithful wife.

This masculine view is in stark contrast to the normal view of a woman. She typically sees sex as a byproduct of *the* relationship. Her sexual stimulation is derived from emotional closeness and bonding with the one man in her life.

Her idea is that sexual intimacy originates from a relationship, not that sex produces a relationship.

Women's sexual encounters result from their emotional and spiritual attachments to *one* significant partner. Therefore, wives have great difficulty understanding the male perspective because it is in such contradistinction to theirs. Seldom will you hear a wife admit that her affair was just a casual, sexual liaison with no emotional attachments to the partner.

These two contrasting perspectives give rise to significant challenges for the individual when he or she begins making reparation for their infidelity in the marriage. Men, please understand this axiom: Your wife will not be comforted if you tell her that your extramarital sex really didn't mean anything to you. You must approach her on the level of her perspective and emotionality. Do not play the "she meant nothing to me" card when referring to your partner in adultery.

Women have said that instead of helping them understand their husband's infidelity, these statements about his emotional disconnection from the other woman angered them. They have asked how their husbands could be so reckless as to risk their marriage on someone who meant nothing to them. Wives equate these careless statements from their husband with what they now assume is his view of her and their marriage: "I must also mean nothing to my husband. He is just responding to his physical urges when we have sex without regard to with whom he is having sex. He is probably fantasizing about another woman."

Couples recovering from an affair must be prepared to work all the way through the process if they want the marriage fully restored. No one can guarantee that the marriage will be saved (see chapter eighteen). Sometimes the offender is not willing to repent, and sometimes the offended is not willing to forgive. However, you will never know unless you make the effort to redeem the marriage with the scriptural principles and processes offered in this book.

While I will refer to certain postulates and principles of psychology, you will not be inundated with unnecessary clinical terminology. Secular psychology affords us an extremely viable and useful glossary of terms describing the spectrum of human behavior. It is this author's view that, while this field of study has provided a valid system for the diagnosing of a problem, it falls palpably short in offering adequate solutions for the "soul" (Greek, *psyche*). To its credit, psychology does not attempt to identify or resolve the needs of the "spirit" (Greek, *pneuma*) of man.

Therefore, our authoritative text for dealing with marital crises and human behavior will be the words of the One who originally designed and engineered the ultimate ideals for mankind and marriage. He answers to the monony "God."

The references to the erring spouse in this book can apply to either a man or woman. For the sake of clarity and simplicity, the unfaithful spouse will be called "Prodigal" and the faithful spouse will be called "Betrayed." Any singular pronouns used for Prodigal, Betrayed, or the new lover will be "he or she"

rivalry

"And he said, A certain man had two sons" (Luke 15:11).

I first focused on the term "Abraham Maslow's Hierarchy of Needs" while attending a class in abnormal psychology. My instructor, a graduate assistant named Andy, wrote the five strata of basic needs on the chalkboard in preparation for the lively discussion that would ensue. He listed these needs in descending order:

1. Physiological

2. Safety

3. Love/Affection

4. Esteem and

5. Self-Actualization

I immediately concluded that my greatest "need" was making an A in this course in order to retain my financial grant. In my somewhat skewed and subjective opinion, my need fit into all five categories. This made my need greater than all of the other students' needs. Isn't that the way it is with our needs? They always seem to be greater than those of others and always seem to teeter on the totter of "life and death."

Sometime later, as I was doing my graduate studies, I was introduced to another highly significant list. This one was called "The Eight Trouble-Spots of Marriage." Since I was now married, I knew I had single-handedly discovered at least *twenty-five*, with a few more "trouble-spots" that were considered borderline. I was anxious to see how someone could trim the list down to just eight and still do justice to the category.

This list identifies these eight trouble-spots as

1. Money Management

2. Anger Management

3. Sexual Differences

4. In-laws

5. Religion

6. Unrealistic Expectations

7. Discipline Decisions, and

8. Domestic Duties

Let's take a look at each of these a little more closely. These will be very brief introductions to these areas of possible conflict in marriage.

Money Management is not a problem for the excessively rich or the desperately poor. The former has more money than they can spend, and the latter doesn't earn enough to have anything left over. It is the group of middle-class couples that have some discretionary funds remaining after the bills are paid that can have conflicts over how or on whom the money will be spent. Will it be golf clubs or a sewing machine, Hi-Def TV or open a savings account? How couples manage their money is the number one arena where arguments arise.

One area of potential conflict is the decision by one of the spouses to maintain a separate checking account. While there may be some valid reasons stemming from poor credit or previous examples of mismanagement or malfeasance where this would be necessary, it should not be seen as conducive to marital oneness. When done for the wrong reasons, it can lead to an inordinate desire to retain individuality and independence apart from the spouse's interference.

This behavior may elicit suspicion, detachment, and distrust in the couple's relationship. Since money management is the number one trouble-spot in marriage, keeping separate accounts will not lend itself (no pun intended) to developing a collective management style for mutual financial accountability.

Decisions regarding household finances should always be a joint effort whenever possible. How much is earned and how it is spent must be mutually discussed and agreed upon if friction and/or resentment are to be avoided. Like many other couples, my wife and I agreed early in our marriage that, when we were blessed with children, she would not work outside the home. Providing the proper *home* environment for our children was of greater priority to us than the value of the *house* we lived in.

This joint decision served us well when we went through periods of financial struggle. Neither of us put blame on the other for our less-than-luxurious lifestyle. We battled the *problem*, not each other. The welfare of our sons was more important to us than mortgaging their future emotional, physical, and spiritual well-being.

We invested our time in them, not in a career for their mother. In the early years as they advanced through school, their mom (and many times Dad) was there to have morning devotions with Jeremy and Jason. We used this time before school to prepare them spiritually for their day. Then came their field trips, ballgames, school plays, and homework, where we were actively involved. Our sons were not "latch-key" kids with a TV as a nanny.

While this decision to be a one-income family affected our bank balance, it did not diminish the spiritual and emotional balance of our home. We did not have the privilege of buying high dollar, brand-name items of clothing or furniture, yet we found that we never did without the things we needed.

We saved all the money we might have spent on family counseling, drug rehabs, booze, bail, tobacco, court fines, divorce lawyers, tutors, and juvenile detentions for items that had the prefixes "faux, gently used, one-owner, irregular, slightly soiled, factory second, store brands, crushed box, overstock, 'Lettuce-patch' dolls, or Air *Johnson* sneakers." We may have lacked some luxuries, but we never lacked the time to be involved in our sons' lives.

The second trouble-spot is Anger Management. How a couple handles their conflicts will greatly determine the survival potential for the marriage. The *goal* of conflicts is to resolve differences of opinion that exist between the spouses. Therefore, the *purpose* of a conflict is not the process or anger management but the reaching of a resolution and an agreement. It is not about winning; it is about learning how to communicate effectively during disagreements.

Anger is generally expressed by one of two ways: People tend to either ventilate or internalize their emotions. The ventilator *blows up* or explodes, spewing his or her toxic tantrum on anyone around. These explosions may include physical as well as the aforementioned verbal tirade. It is not unusual for these "hotheads" to kick the cat, slam the door, or throw an object during their rant. As a rule, explosions are followed by a calming of the anger and a reversion to their more normal behavior.

The internalizer *bottles up* their emotions. They don't yell, kick, or scream. They may just do a slow burn for several days. Their behavior is marked by withdrawal from intimacy and interaction with little or no explanation. When pressed, they may even say that nothing is wrong. However, it is apparent to the spouse that something is very wrong; they just don't have a clue as to what they have done to trigger this bottling up of emotions in their companion. At some point, the angry internalizer either finally speaks up or simply outlasts their anger and decides to move on emotionally.

Just to conclude this very basic introduction to Anger Management, it is critical for you to understand that *neither* of these reactions is a viable option for the Christian couple. Here is what God says about each of these exaggerated and improper behavioral responses. To the ventilator, He says in Ephesians 4:15 that they must speak the truth *in love*. To the internalizer, God says in Ephesians 4:26, "Be ye angry, and sin not: let not the *sun go down* upon your wrath." What God is teaching here is Basic Anger Management. He demands composure and decorum in the way we handle our anger as an expression of our Christian discipline. Deal with it properly and deal with it now, not later, is God's recipe for peace in life and marriage.

The third trouble-spot for couples involves the Sexual Dynamics of their marriage. Much could be said here about the physiological, psychological, spiritual, and emotional attributes that affect a person's sexuality and, therefore, the sexual climate of the marriage. Obviously, it is listed third because it is a major cause of marital discord.

Many husbands actually consider sexual differences to

be the primary contributor to dissatisfaction and dysfunction in their marriage. More accurately, it is probably the primary barometer depicting that there *is* dysfunction in the marriage. Sex is certainly not a subject that needs to be ignored but addressed and corrected; nor should it be used as a reward or punishment. Well, maybe as a reward, but *never* for punitive purposes.

There are many good books on the market that deal exclusively with this area of a couple's relationship, and I would encourage you to invest in one if you need help in educating yourself in the science of human sexuality. In order to properly deal with the problems of sex, you need to understand that men and women view and approach sex from entirely different perspectives. Think in terms of the North Pole and South Pole or fire and ice or night and day as representing these differences of perspective. Therefore, the more you learn about each other, the more you become intellectually and emotionally intimate, the more you will see your level of physical intimacy improve in your marriage.

Dr. Richard Dobson, Director of Emerge Ministries, has stated that of all the couples who have come to his office for counseling, he has never seen a couple that demonstrated two specific qualities. The first is an uninhibited prayer life, and the other is an uninhibited sex life.

When a couple can pray together without fear, inferiority, or hang-ups, and when they can engage in sex without fear, inferiority, or hang-ups, they have the two greatest ingredients working for them in their marriage. When problems arise, they can pray them out or love them out; thus, they will seldom need professional help.

Number four on the trouble-spot list is In-laws. As one comedian once said, "In-laws ought to be outlawed!" That view might find many supporters. However, in-laws come with the marriage. Whether they are close in proximity or distant, whether active or passive in your marriage, whether dead or alive, your in-laws will have an impact on your marriage. The reason is that your spouse probably lived with them longer than he or she has lived with you. Certainly, their formative years, when their views and values were shaped, were spent under the impact of their parents or guardians.

Each of you has been programmed in certain areas of your life to react or to respond as you learned from your parents' influence on you. Your values, priorities, lifestyle, attitudes, and emotional responses have all been shaped by what you saw in your parents' home. So, even if they are not near physically, their presence will still make itself known in your marriage. Now, should they live close or meddle in your marriage, you will definitely discover that the lines of allegiance can get blurred very quickly, and one of you may feel that you are on the outside of the family circle looking in.

Moving down the list, we come to number five, Religious Differences. This one sometimes comes with gunfire! After all, societies are infamous for killing people who do not agree with their religious tenets. Major wars have started and some continue currently with the root of the hostility being a matter of religious intolerance. Couples with radically different religious views who think they can avoid this collision course are sadly mistaken.

These religious differences are not just restricted to the major areas, like whether one is Catholic and one Protestant or whether one is Christian and the other is Jewish. Religious differences will surface on such subjects as tithing, frequency of church attendance, Bible versions, which denomination to attend, which style of worship service is preferred, who leads family devotions, whether to have family devotions, how active will you be in your church, and many other situations that can arise.

Because religion, like sex, is such a personal matter, couples can find themselves at odds over how to address the challenges that come in these areas. Even though this is somewhat down the list, it is by no means inconsequential. There can be real causalities of war from the failure to handle your religious differences properly.

Unrealistic Expectations appears at number six on our trouble-spot list. What exactly does "unrealistic expectations" mean? Everyone has things he or she imagines the marriage will manifest. Many of these anticipations are well within the normal range of expectation for the couple. However, the realm of fantasy can overtake the reasonable probabilities and create a disproportionate level of dissatisfaction when they do not materialize.

This can happen when one or both of the spouses assume that the surreal atmosphere of the wedding day will be the norm for the day-to-day grind of marriage. It can be a rude awakening when the bride discovers that the groom does not wear a tuxedo every day and he realizes he will never see her in her gown again. She may find that he may never carry her over the threshold again and probably will cease opening the car door for her soon. He may discover that the reception was the last time she let him kiss her in public or take her garter off.

The most common misconception in the first years of a marriage is the underestimation or overestimation of the spouse's sex drive. This misconception leads to unrealistic expectations for the husband as he discovers that their romance and sexual frequency will start cooling shortly after marriage. The bride will find that he no longer engages in those long conversations they used to have before marriage.

Just as the spouses may demonstrate different opinions on sexual frequency, he or she may also differ on what should be appropriate for the lovemaking menu. What is allowed or disallowed by one of the spouses has spawned innumerable arguments in the bedroom that can lead to acrimony in the courtroom. It is usually the more conservative spouse who demands he or she get his or her way in setting the boundaries for acceptable sexual activity in the marriage.

To demonstrate this dilemma, I use my following analogy to help the partners see it from a different, less confrontational, non-threatening perspective.

Let us imagine that someone grows up hearing about how wonderful it is to eat ice cream. He or she has been told that, no matter how delicious and refreshing it is, he or she will have to wait until the time is right before indulging in the dessert. When he or she becomes an adult, he or she is told he or she will be able to enjoy this treat, without guilt, for the rest of his or her life. All along the way, he or she hears songs, reads articles, views movies, and sees advertisements displaying how great ice cream is going to be.

He or she even has friends his or her own age who have sneaked around and gotten a few scoops without their parents' knowledge. These friends can't wait to brag about their surreptitious sundaes that ushered them into adulthood. The more he or she hears about ice cream, the more it intrigues and interests him or her. He or she becomes enamored by the colors, the flavors, the textures, the taste; even the fat content interests him or her. In fact, he or she seems consumed with getting some as soon as he or she possibly can. However, the legal and moral prerequisites for going scooping are, "You must be married."

Eventually, he or she gets to the point in life where he or

she has found someone who really appeals to them and they decide to get married. With all of the wonderful attributes the sweetheart has going for him or her, he or she discovers that the greatest part of the marriage is the realization that the spouse owns *a creamery*. This is simply too good to be true!

To think that you have dreamed of ice cream since adolescence and now your life's companion owns a creamery is beyond ecstasy. Finally, your obsession with ice cream will be satisfied because you can now go hang out at the creamery anytime you wish. It will be such a temptation to think about the creamery all day long and how you cannot wait to go visit again. Sometimes, you may find yourself thinking more about the creamery than you do your sweetheart.

After you marry, you quickly discover that your spouse is much more proprietary about his or her creamery than you expected. He or she has never permitted *loitering* and probably has never allowed trespassers to come on the premises. What you thought was going to be your "second home" is now starting to appear a little less hospitable. It is becoming obvious that it will take time and many intimate and intense discussions in order to tool out the policies and procedures for visiting hours.

Because you have longed for this time in your life when you could enjoy unlimited access to the ice cream container, you are quite surprised to discover that your views are not necessarily shared. However, the real shock surfaces when you tell your spouse, the CEO of the creamery, that you *like* vanilla, but you have *longed* to try some "snicker doodle," or "cinnamon dulce de leche," or "black raspberry chip," or even a hearty helping of some "strawberry" once in a while. How rebuffed and ridiculed you feel when you are told, "*This creamery* does not cater to those deviant and unnatural taste buds."

It is not uncommon that a real ice cream connoisseur like

yourself or your spouse discovers all too late that your mate is a disciple of the "vanilla only" philosophy, and that is the *only* flavor he or she offers. How belittling it is when your spouse, the creamery CEO, pontificates, "This creamery permits only one flavor, the *right* flavor, God's flavor, and it will never change, so get over it. You can fantasize about what's in other people's cones all you want, but *that stuff don't cook in my kitchen.*"

When this mirrors the circumstances in their marriage, I cautiously advise, "Try to keep a 'Good Humor Man,' or it may be a 'Rocky Road' ahead for a while!"

With this possibility of such differing perspectives, it is therefore *unrealistic* for either party to assume that there will not be changes in the behavior of their spouse after marriage. "Courtship conduct" and "marriage conduct" are seldom the same. There certainly may be some "cause/effect" factors that need to be addressed with the couple's behavior after the honeymoon to help avoid the possibility of a major crisis.

Sometimes the problem is as simple as conflict between supply and demand. He may demand more sex than she can supply. For the new wife, it is not uncommon for her to suffer from a condition called dyspareunia, which means "difficult or painful sexual intercourse." This is a situation in which the loving husband should respond with extreme tenderness and patience. Medical help may be needed if the symptoms continue to diminish the wife's ability to enjoy intimacy with her husband. It definitely should not be ignored by either party.

Discipline Decisions appears as number seven on our list. This problem concerns which person in the marriage actually "rules the roost." In the animal kingdom, it is not unusual for the female to be the dominant gender and the male to be the subordinate one. There are some species where the female actually kills the male after their offspring are born. This behavior eliminates any chance of power struggles in the relationship. Thankfully, there are laws that prohibit wives from resorting to this extreme conduct in today's society.

This category addresses the conflicts that can arise over *who* makes the decisions in the family. As a rule, most couples will collaborate before making significant decisions, and they will come to a consensus of opinion as to the proper course of action. These could include decisions such as what time you arise, when do you go to bed, what time you have your meals, how often you attend church, who controls the TV remote, or what style of corrective measures you use with the children, just to name a few. Remember, it is not so much what decisions are made but by whom the decisions are made!

Finishing the list of the eight potential trouble-spots is Domestic Duties. In some ways, this is a continuation of the previous trouble-spot. The conflicts this category refers to are the perfunctory, day-to-day responsibilities of the couple. Those would include areas such as who fixes the meals and who cleans the kitchen; which one will do the laundry; which has to bathe the children; who mows the lawn; or who vacuums the house. Basically, here we deal with who does the work around the house.

These duties all require someone to make a decision. The rub comes in when it is not a collaborative effort between the couple but an edict from an *emperor*. Though this category is at the bottom of the list, it is still a "fly in the ointment" of many marriages. No individual wants to feel that he or she is a slave to the dictates of his or her partner with no input into the daily routine of the household.

Neither does anyone want to feel that their gender has predisposed them to a disparate number of responsibilities being considered theirs. In marriage, there really is no such thing as "women's work" and "men's work"; it is all "couple's work." *How* the couple decides on the division of labor is more critical to the success of the marriage than *who* performs a specific task.

More than a few brides have had to schedule some serious re-orientation for their husband when they discovered that he considered the perfect wife as "one who looks like a woman, acts like a lady, thinks like a man, and works like a dog!" Socrates once said, "If you get a good wife you will be happy; if you get a bad one you will become a philosopher." It is not uncommon that a masculine attitude adjustment is necessary.

The goal here is for agreement in these eight aforementioned areas as to what are the *best* procedures for the couple to follow that produce the *best* results. After a candid discussion of the situation, someone will need to defer to the wisdom of the other. Husbands, do not feel insulted if your wife has a better grasp of household management than you do. That is fairly normal in today's society.

A later cataloging of marriage problems I found synthesized them into a list of these three: (1) Money, (2) Obnoxious Behavior (where twenty-three of mine originated), and (3) Sex. It is evident from these lists that the *ecstasy* of marriage can meet head-on with the *agony* of reality when the marriage fails to live up to the blissful anticipation of the honeymooning couple.

Everyone has needs, and you will see this referenced frequently in this book. While the list could become a compendium of human dysfunctions and neuroses, our plan is to keep it as simple as possible without doing a disservice to the very real needs we all have.

Many marriage specialists agree that the number one need of a man is *admiration*. Ladies, your man will never outgrow nor outlive his need to be admired. A man will jump out of airplanes, scale mountains, race cars, become a workaholic, place his bowling trophies on the coffee table, mount a moose head over the fireplace, display deer antlers over the loveseat, or any number of things just so someone will see his accomplishments and give him an "attaboy."

Admiration means the most to a husband when it comes from his wife. However, men will gladly accept kudos from others also—just make sure that it isn't another woman who shows more admiration to your husband than you. The overwhelming testimonial of wayward men is that it was not the physical beauty of the other woman that made them vulnerable to infidelity; it was the way she treated him and how she made him feel about himself that led him astray.

We have learned that there are three major needs inherent in both men and women: acceptance, appreciation, and approval. From the Queen of England to her lowly scrubwoman, people everywhere long for these three forms of affirmation. You can *never* give too much affirmation to your loved ones.

For most men, the conveying of approval tops the list. They see approval as embracing the other two qualities of acceptance and appreciation because of how it makes them feel about themselves. Nowhere is this situation more evident than where it is addressed in Proverbs 7:10–21. There Solomon warns the young men to be vigilant regarding the tactics a prostitute will use to capture her clients.

The enticement begins with

1. Offering him an "all-night sex marathon." This appeals to his sense of manhood and virility. It is, in actuality, a physical impossibility for him since his body usually requires at least forty-five

minutes to recover and recycle sexually before
he can continue. Her first advance is designed
to stimulate his *imagination*.

Men have always attributed peculiar significance to the semen
their body ejaculates. Hippocrates and others from antiquity
commented on its "precious" character. Pythagoras called it "the
flower of the blood." Some called it an emanation of the brain,
and Epicurus described it as a product of the soul rather than
the body. As late as the turn of the twentieth century, medical
textbooks declared that the loss of an ounce of semen equaled
the loss of forty ounces of blood. They concluded that "excessive
(whatever that may be) intercourse" leads to ill health.

In a medieval document by Moses ben Maimon (1135–1204),
it is stated,

He who immerses himself in sexual intercourse will be
assailed by premature aging. His strength will wane,
his eyes will weaken and a bad odor will emit from his
mouth and armpits. His teeth will fall out and many
other maladies will afflict him. The wise physicians have
stated that one in 1,000 die from illness and the remaining 999 from excessive sexual intercourse. Therefore, a
man must be cautious in this matter if he wishes to live
wholesomely. He should not cohabit unless his body is
healthy and very strong, and he experiences many invol-
untary erections. Such a person requires coitus and it is
therapeutic for him.

It would not be unusual for both husbands and wives to agree
in principle with these overviews of sexual intimacy. The
husbands will quickly agree that their emissions are "special

and mandatory," while many wives might describe their husbands as "needing a shower *and* out of their minds."

2. The "temptation thermostat" increases to another level when she offers him a glimpse into her boudoir. The prostitute knows the importance of utilizing the Five Sensory Responses to snare her man. Now she is working on his senses of *sight and touch*. The seductress tells him of her ornate bedroom with imported linen sheets and her scantily clad body awaiting his entrance.

3. Solomon warns that she will quickly proceed to the next level, which is to lure him further through his sense of *smell*. She describes the aromatic atmosphere of her bedroom as being enhanced by myrrh, aloes, and cinnamon. All of these expensive fragrances were to be used for his primal need of sexual satisfaction. Can you imagine how admired she made him feel as she spared no expense for his enjoyment?

4. A good hunter knows you do not stop baiting the prey until you have him snared. The prostitute moves in for the kill by employing the next level of her enticement strategy. She knows what he wants to *hear*. Proverbs next tells us she whispers "seductive speech and coaxing flatteries" in his ear. No nagging or complaining would come from her lips.

   Men have often been accused of being terrible listeners, but that all changes when you start talking about sex. She knew what would pierce his resistance and make him vulnerable to her advances. She talked erotic, hardcore sex to him and was getting ready to "reel him in."

5.   Just to make sure that her time had not been wasted, Solomon stated she would further her sexual safari by adding another level to her arsenal. She aimed the next major sortie at his *ego*. The prostitute tells him just how much she wants him as her sexual partner. She does not use ambiguity or veiled references as to what she has in mind for him and his personal satisfaction. Her last words assure him that her desire is *for him* and no one else. She is telling him that it would be *easy* for him to get her in bed.

6.   In her skilled and cunning way, she has saved the most powerful weapon for last. The prostitute of Proverbs 7 moves to the last level and appeals to his sense of *taste*. Solomon says she sealed the deal of enticement by "kissing him." This would not have been a mere peck on the cheek. This would have been a full-blown, passionate, taste-my-tonsils kind of kiss. In the anatomical field of science, a kiss is described as "the juxtaposition of two obicularis oris muscles in a state of contraction."

While contemplating the ecstasy of this romantic convergence, an ancient Egyptian lyricist once penned these insightful words: "If I embrace her and her arms are open, I am like a man in the land of perfumes. If I kiss her and her lips are open, I am drunk even without beer." Can anyone improve on that passionate perspective from centuries past?

Sadly, when this illicit strategy of enticement by the prostitute works, as it did with this young man, Solomon describes the epilogue of the events as leading to his "execution." Verse 22 says, "He followed her as an ox going to the butcher." Many marriages have been "butchered" because a husband allowed his need for admiration to be fulfilled by someone other than his wife. Husbands and wives, take counsel from Solomon; the needs of men are *real* but must only be satisfied by a caring, informed, and attentive wife. Men, there can be no other options allowed if you want to stay away from the slaughterhouse!

Wives who wish to be "informed" can use Solomon's overview of the prostitute's tactics to help satisfy adequately their husband's basic emotional and physical needs. He reveals the reasons the illicit strategy of the prostitute is so successful in its seduction. Now, the devoted wife can be armed with the plan of the "professionals." She can use it lovingly and legitimately to fill a need in her husband without the threat of a *slaughterhouse* hanging over his head.

From this text, we conclude the following five things a husband needs from his wife:

1. She *desires* him

2. She *shows her attraction to him and makes advances* toward him

3. She *openly flirts* with him

4. She makes intentional, aggressive, *uninhibited sexual overtures* toward him, and

5. She is *easily available* for lovemaking.

These are some of the more attractive attributes a man desires in his wife. The husband will not mind his wife burning the biscuits if she will make sure their marriage bed is *on fire* also!

To the skilled behaviorist, it seems evident that the number one need of a woman is *security*. By this, we refer to emotional security. Probably a better working definition for security would be the word "devotion." While most women appreciate the finer things in life, like crystal stemware, fine china, linen tablecloths, and silverware, they are often willing to forfeit these dainty, frilly, soft, or expensive items for an environment of love and devotion from their husbands. Women long to be emotionally bonded with their mates, not just cohabit physically.

Women love to be complimented on their appearance. A female counselee once complained that she now "had wrinkles in places where there used to not be *places.*" We all want to grow old, but no one wants to look old. No matter what her age, one of the last things a wife wants from her husband is a verbal makeover. This process has been called "the Pygmalion Effect."

According to mythology, Pygmalion, King of Cyprus, sculpted a female statue out of ivory and named it Galatea. She was created to represent the perfect specimen of womanhood. The king fashioned Galatea just as he wanted his woman to be down to the finest detail. He was her architect and left no detail to the imagination. He was so smitten with the beauty of his creation that he fell in love with her and prayed to the goddess of love, Aphrodite, to bring her to life so he could enjoy her.

Mythology, like its cousin Heresy, usually contains only an element of truth, which makes both of them much more attractive and embraceable for their audiences. What is the truth that lies embedded in Pygmalion's story as it relates to couples today?

Many modern wives demonstrate a "Galatea Complex" and feel that the man they are married to really does come from the family of "*pig*-malions." They believe their husbands will never be satisfied with them as they are, because "their king" is constantly trying to change them into someone or something they are not. He always has his chisel handy and keeps chipping away at his wife.

It seems that some husbands believe the Bible instructs them to "train up a *wife* in the way she should go ... " (see Proverbs 22:6). Actually, that is exactly what the Bible elsewhere commands a husband to do. However, there is a context in which that is to take place, and we must investigate what the collective Scriptures require of the husband.

For this very sensitive subject, let's look at Ephesians 5:28–29. First of all, Paul tells the husbands *what* to do. He establishes the nature of the process by informing the husbands that they "ought to love their wives as they love their own bodies." The Greek word used here for *ought* means "to owe as a debt or an obligation." The great apostle tells husbands that they actually owe it to their wives to love them with the same degree that they love and care for themselves. When you do not do this, Paul says, "Husbands, you are being delinquent in paying the debt you owe to your wife by not loving her as you should."

The Apostle Peter gives further straightforward directions to husbands of all ages in 1 Peter 3:7, where he says, "Likewise, ye husbands, dwell with *them* according to knowledge, giving honour unto the wife, as unto the weaker vessel, and as being heirs together of the grace of life; that your prayers be not hindered" (emphasis mine). At the heart of growing together as a couple is the need for each spouse to have specific knowledge of *how* to demonstrate love to their companion.

It is an axiom of counseling that states many people may be suffering from apathy toward their spouses, not because they don't know *what* to do, but because of a lack of knowledge as to *how* to do it. I have found that many do not know what to do or how to do it. Therefore, the best counseling method for them is a didactic one where they are *taught* the principles of a successful marriage.

The word *knowledge* used in the Bible is usually the translation of one of two Greek words. The first Greek word refers to what we would call "*innate* knowledge." This is knowledge that comes from the heart, having been placed there by God without the assistance of an educational process. In religious jargon, it is often referred to as "revelation knowledge."

The second Greek word refers to knowledge that is gained from experience, either yours or other's. It is *acquired* knowledge or experiential knowledge. It is the latter alternative that Peter uses in his directive to husbands. The injunction is for the husband to gain all the knowledge he can about *his* wife and then incorporate this in his attitudes and conduct toward her. Peter says to fail at this divine mandate will cause self-imposed spiritual suffering for the husband.

Failure on this level may quickly cause your loving relationship to turn into a bitter rivalry. What started as a *duet* can sadly dissolve into a *duel*. It only takes two people in a relationship to establish whether they will compete with or compliment one another. Acquired knowledge of your partner will help you avoid the tragedy of having the harmony of your duet turn into the cacophony of a duel when your rapport turns to rivalry.

The following words are one of the verses to the song I wrote and recorded for my wife as a surprise anniversary gift. It was my way of expressing to her my commitment to always keep love's flames burning brightly in our hearts and marriage.

Times can be cruel, make lovers duel, cause them to go seperate ways,
Make true love sour, like old faded flowers, forgetting their happier days,

But in our glad times, and even in our sad times, nothing can drive us apart,
We'll not betray our wedding day, that's when I gave you my heart.

"Abbie's Song" (copyright 1993)

2

requisition

"Give me my portion now!" (Luke 15:12)

How should a husband love his wife? The answer is simple: like she *wants and needs* to be loved. Never have I had a male counselee who knew the five kinds of love that a woman needs. This instruction from Peter in chapter one regarding gaining knowledge must not go unheeded. Therefore, significant portions of the first conjoint counseling sessions were comprised of educating the couple in the science and art of marriage. We always began by describing the five special love needs of the wife.

The first love need is Companionship Love. Women are by nature predisposed toward bonding. They do not make good hermits. Isolation is like a death sentence for them. Therefore, they form deep, lasting friendships where companionship is preeminent. Women forge many relationships that are satisfying, but the one they desire the greatest is that their husband become an emotional companion, not just a physical companion.

Wives believe that becoming "one" starts with emotional

bonding that springs from open, transparent involvement with each other. An insightful definition used in archaic English described companionship as "eating together." When you took the time to share a meal with someone, you were showing them their sense of worth to you.

The second love need in women is for Compassionate Love. Women have the capacity to express love, care, and concern for people who are suffering. They make tremendous caregivers and nurses. What husbands sometimes fail to realize is her need to be cared for or nursed when she is ill or tired. The calloused husband who walks in the room where his sick wife has spent the day grappling with the symptoms of PMS or the flu will find little tolerance when his first remarks are to inquire as to what she has prepared for dinner. Men, show your wife the same type of compassion she shows you or your children when you are under the weather.

The third love need is called Affectionate Love. Because men are typically restrained in their expressions of emotion, this area can become a problem early on in the marriage. Affection involves handholding, tender and loving words, long walks together, sitting together on the couch, cards, flowers, and various other demonstrations of the depths of feeling that he has for her. Women crave this kind of love from their man because it is non-invasive, non-demanding, and appeals to her need to be liked and loved when not in the bedroom.

The fourth need is Romantic Love. Women never outgrow their need for romance. Do you wonder why romance novels are some of the largest selling books in the publishing industry? Those books give vicarious enjoyment to women whose personal need for romance is unfulfilled. Ladies love dining out, not just eating out. They find great satisfaction in a husband who will cater to their innate desire for soft, romantic music, lace tablecloths, linen napkins, dinner by candlelight, and the ecstasy of being "courted" after marriage. Cards, flowers, and candy can reap unbelievable responses from your sweetheart when you initiate romantic gestures just for her.

The fifth love need is Passionate Love. Given the opportunity, most men would skip one through four and head straight for number five. Men do not need small talk, caregiving, handholding, foot rubs, flowers, chocolates, or fine dining to become passionate. Because men do not need these things in order to be stimulated, they incorrectly assume that women do not need them either. That is a basic flaw in the thinking of husbands.

Husbands are sexually stimulated either by the sight of a beautiful woman or by the absence of a recent sexual experience. For many husbands, a "teddy" lingerie outfit has replaced the dog as man's best friend. Women, on the other hand, need to have their emotional fires *stoked* before they are ready to begin lovemaking.

Women want passion, not just a physical experience. Passion must be ignited in the heart of a wife if she is to *desire* sexual intimacy. Intimacy, for her, is the logical conclusion of the companionship, compassion, affection, and romance her husband has shown her throughout the day. Men, if you want her to give you number five, start early in the morning giving ample expressions of numbers one through four to your wife.

In Ephesians 5:29, Paul instructs husbands on exactly *how* they are to accomplish this rather risky responsibility. He uses two words to describe the methodology for paying the debt men owe their wives. First, he must *nourish* his wife. This Greek word means "to nurture and nourish to maturity." The word is used only twice in the New Testament. It projects the same idea as that of a mother tenderly and lovingly caring for her child who is the object of her affection and attention. A mother's love is tender and selfless. This is the way a husband should love and nourish his wife.

The last word Paul uses to describe how a husband can pay his debt to his wife is the word "cherish." It literally means "to keep warm, comfort, use tender love and care, to have and to hold." Too many women complain that their husbands only want to *have* them but seldom just *hold* them. The wife wants and needs both. Probably the most practical application of the word "cherish" means "to pamper." Most women have a pretty good idea of what "pamper" means, and they love the idea of their husbands adoring them enough to pamper them.

There is something about that word that captures the imagination of a woman's heart. She desperately wants to be pampered. God knew this, Paul knew this, and now, men, you know this. Paul tells these first-century husbands that they have a debt they owe their wives. God confirms this principle by saying this is how "one-flesh" marriages are established. Men, if you will be the husband you are supposed to be by loving, nourishing, and cherishing your wife, she will become the wife you need her to be. This is God's divine order, and it starts with the husband's treatment of his wife.

A wife will excuse a lot of your sins of omission if she sees you are trying to pamper her. Husbands, your clumsiness, tardiness, sloppiness, forgetfulness, or busyness will register only slightly on her Richter scale of potential eruption if you show her that you simply want to spend the evening pampering her. All women want to be cherished. If you aren't sure how to begin, just ask your wife and she will gladly point you in the right direction. It usually has its origin in the kitchen, followed by the clothes hamper, emptying the trash, or some other, less than romantic, mundane task.

Men usually think of pampering as a "bedroom activity," but it certainly does not begin there; never has and never will. You must start where she can see that your efforts are purely and solely for *her* benefit. You must be totally altruistic, not narcissistic, in your motives. Your wife will be naturally suspicious if you are doing a 180-degree turn from the normal "quid pro quo" behavior of husbands who often barter for sex from their wives. This pampering cannot have even the slightest hint of a bribe.

What is "quid pro quo," you ask? It is a Latin term used primarily in legal circles and carries the meaning of "something for something" or, as in our application, "this for that." It is a bargaining tool used to negotiate an agreement. It means you will provide *this* if the other party will provide *that*. Most men do not seem to have a clue as to what the "this" their wife desires is, but they certainly know what the "that" they want from their wife is. In marriage, there can be a great dependence on this proviso, because marriage can appear like such an uneven playing field. It is not uncommon for spouses to look for ways to level the situation by using their bargaining ability to its maximum benefit.

This method of negotiation is common in the workplace. However, it is far from being the kind of love that Paul refers to in his writing. That love was called *agape* in Greek, and it conveyed a "self-sacrificing," "other-oriented" nature to it. *Agape* is also referred to as "the God-kind" of love. This is a "quid only" kind of love. It means God offers us *this* without demanding *that* from us. The world isn't accustomed to this type of love, so it can seem foreign to the uninitiated. It is the purest and noblest of the four types of love referred to in the Greek language and referenced in the Bible.

Men, when you do not take time to be with your wife, pamper her in a nonsexual context, and listen to her, you are doing a great disservice to both her and yourself. Prudent husbands have learned that the fastest way to a woman's body is through her heart. Voltaire said, "The road to the heart is the ear." Open up and talk, but listen also. Really listen, and she will *feel* loved by you. Paul Tillich says, "The first duty of love is to listen."

The best way for you to listen to your wife is with your *eyes*. Look at her attentively when she is speaking. Communication experts tell us that the intensity of listening can be measured by the degree of eye contact made with the speaker. Eye contact shows you are interested in the speaker and the subject. Eye contact compliments the speaker by showing your interest and attention. During courtship, prolonged eye contact is deemed the most important nonsexual gesture made by the couple. Sadly, it seems to diminish after marriage

Men, your wife wants your attention. When you give it freely, she will feel secure in your love. Unfortunately, if she finds someone else more interested in her, who hangs on every word she speaks, she may become vulnerable to his advances. It has been stated that women can speak at the rate of approximately 140 words per minute with *gusts* up to about 180. Therefore, husbands, you must be active, passionate listeners if you are to keep up with what your wife is saying. Husbands, do not allow any other man to "out-listen" you when your wife is speaking.

The Song of Solomon provides a wonderful paradigm for marital love. Throughout the eight chapters of this salacious saga, the couple is *mutually* engaged in deep, thoughtful, intimate, transparent conversation … with one another! He or she lets his or her guard down, he or she opens up to one another, he or she expresses his or her feelings and desires, and he or she does not play "mind games."

Most women do not find this type of open and unguarded communication unusual. They seem quite comfortable "baring their souls" to their trusted friends. Men see friendship as "activities," such as making or doing things, while women see it as a "sharing" experience. Sociologist Andrew Greeley once said, "The basic ingredients for a good marriage are friendship and sex."

It most often appears to be the man who has the greater difficulty opening up about his feelings. Too much of the "machismo" cultural influence has persuaded the man that he must be tough, guarded, noncommunicative, and emotionally detached from others. Men have trouble expressing their desires and feelings unless they are negative emotions, such as anger, jealousy, or frustration. Their self-image of toughness will only allow them to emote within the sphere of this "John Wayne Syndrome" with the stereotypical conduct of ignoring the girl and kissing his horse.

A cursory overview of the Song of Solomon will reveal that this particular man did some deliberate and specific romantic talking as a prelude to any intimacy that would follow. Every word he spoke regarding his feelings for his bride deepened his love for her, her love for him, and the accompanying mutual feelings of security and intimacy in the relationship.

She sensed his devotion to her, and this produced a quantum leap in her visceral responses and reactions to his overtures of love. He talked *to* her *about* her. This is absolutely the ultimate secret formula for romantic success. If you ask any woman what she wishes to hear from her lover, she will tell you that it just doesn't get any better than this!

So what did he say to her that produced such a sense of

security and devotion in her heart toward him? It is all there in black and white in the eight chapters, should you need some coaxing. To be succinct, he *noticed* her! He takes the time to express his pleasure with her. In comparing her with others (a somewhat high-risk maneuver), he makes sure that she is always the standard by which everyone else is judged. Then he assures her that, in his view, *all* other women fall far short of her beauty and perfection.

This man *compliments* his bride's hair, voice, teeth, legs, tummy, nose, ears, feet, lips, cheeks, mouth, neck, and her figure. This was not a "one-time" plunge into his feminine side predicated on ulterior motives. He carefully made sure that he showed his devotion by making this a lifestyle of romantic reassurances for her. The capstone of his conversation is his sincere synopsis given in the Song of Solomon 4:7, where it records these powerful (and productive) words from this man to his bride: "You are so beautiful, my beloved, so perfect in every part" (TLB). How long do you think it took her to invite him into her chamber after he hit that "homerun"?

Men, if you need admiration and expect your wife to provide it for you, you must be willing to acknowledge the need your wife has for *security* (devotion) and be willing to provide this for her. Being open, honest, and transparent in your feelings for one another will be one of the greatest safeguards you can have against the perils of marital discord. Limit your criticisms and be extravagant in your compliments toward one another. Proverbs shows the way a wife can love her husband. The Song of Solomon shows the way a man can love his wife.

Through my interaction with couples in crisis, I have discovered one of the greatest barriers to emotional and physical intimacy in marriage is the "IF Factor." The word "if" represents an acrostic that describes the typical view of the couple's attitude toward communication in marriage.

The "i" stands for *information*. This is a man's primary concept of what a discussion with his wife should be. He usually sees a conversation as an opportunity to collect or to disseminate information or data. Men are into facts! They are, by nature, problem solvers. Therefore, once they have heard the problem and stated the obvious solution, in their minds the conversation is successfully concluded.

It seems, however, that we still have the last letter of "if" to deal with. The "f" represents *feelings*. This is considered "woman's country" by most men. Men really do not understand why their wives would rather discuss feelings than facts. Women view conversations as prime opportunities to share their feelings with others. Men will generally ask "what do you think?" questions, while women will more than likely ask "how do you feel?" questions. This is by no means a criticism of women. It is apparent that a wife wants more out of her husband's conversations than an interrogation followed by a schematic for problem solving.

Because of this inherent gender bias, many marriages begin to disintegrate when the wife discovers that her husband cannot carry on a "decent conversation," and the husband concludes his wife just wants to "avoid a discussion" of the facts. The "If Factor" can be problematic for the marriage as long as the couple fails to realize and respect the perspective of their spouse and seeks ways to adjust their conversation to include *both* information and feelings.

It is in this way that both parties will see conversations in a positive light and will look forward to more times of sharing. A husband can deepen his wife's sense of security by allowing her to emote. A wife can heighten her husband's feelings of admiration by allowing him to talk about facts, data, and problem-solving techniques without censure.

After many years of both pastoral and professional counseling, I have noticed that there is usually a confluence of the eight tributaries previously called "trouble-spots" flowing into what may feel like a raging river of marital discord. Many times the counselee has responded to this list by stating that their marriage exhibited all of them. At this point, we tried to determine what the primary, secondary, and tertiary sources of the disharmony were. Then the process of dealing more efficiently with their concerns can begin.

Effective counseling of any description will involve confronting not only the *symptoms*, but also the *setting* and the *source* of problem. The temptation for many in the "self-help" culture is to focus only on the symptoms they are experiencing.

"Just make the pain go away!" is a common cry by the medical patient or the counseling client. However, proper treatment includes more than just dispensing pain pills. There must be some excavation of the patient's medical or psychological history to determine the setting or the *condition* of the problem.

To be able to understand properly the pathology of the individual, several key questions must be asked by the counselor. First, what are the present *circumstances* that elicit this distress? Second, what is happening in his or her world that makes him or her vulnerable to this present situation? Until he or she unravels some of his or her nurturing and environmental history, he or she may not have a full grasp of the depth of his or her problem. There is another level of unearthing that is most vital to the understanding of what is happening in his or her life. That is the *source* level of his or her feelings and behavior.

A medical example would be someone who experienced pain in his or her foot ("symptoms"). Upon visible examination, a large open wound was seen ("setting"). When the physician performed some basic tests, it was discovered that the patient had diabetes ("source"). It is obvious from this illustration that just taking pain medication or rubbing antibiotic creams on the wound was not going to cure the problem. This would constitute treating the symptoms and the setting. Real help does not begin until you isolate the underlying source of the pain and the wound. Then, proper treatment can begin for the disease.

The source represents the deepest level of diagnosis. It focuses on the origins of our sensitivity to conditions and circumstances. The source is the true *cause* of the problem. What kind of emotional baggage from his or her past is he or she dealing with that produces these feelings or reactions? Something may have originated in early childhood. The source could be painful things that happened to him or her, how he or she saw himself or herself, how he or she was treated by others, or a host of other stimuli. Whatever it is, the *source* is the ultimate reason why one feels and reacts the way he or she does.

The scenarios in this book are gleaned from the stories of numerous counselees in both my church counseling and private practice. His or her identities are protected, and no reference will endanger his or her anonymity. Again, let me remind you that this book is written so the offender and the offended are non-gendered. From my case studies, *it is approximately of equal proportion in the division between straying husbands and unfaithful wives*. Therefore, the references can apply to either an erring man or an erring woman.

The parable of the prodigal ("wasteful") son in Luke 15 gives numerous interesting and appropriate parallels to the circumstances involving marital infidelity. The painful betrayal by a spouse is not a single act but a process of attitudes and actions that can culminate in adultery. Whether the marriage is *destroyed* or *restored* is determined by the commitment of the couple to follow a procedure of healing as outlined in the Bible. The devastation of the present disclosure can be displaced by the jubilant dancing of recovery *if* he or she will use God's portrait of restoration shown in this text.

This biblical account helps answer the haunting questions of why and how such a horrible thing could happen to a Christian couple. It also provides a roadmap for recovery to the couples who seek God's wisdom during the time of his or her greatest crisis. However, the first question that explodes in the mind of the Betrayed is, *Why did Prodigal do this to me?* This question deserves an answer. I hope that we can shed some light on Prodigal's motivation.

The seed for adultery begins germinating in Prodigal's heart when he or she becomes focused on himself or herself. The "culture of narcissism" promotes an egocentric society. Prodigals start making comparisons with others and often views his or her life as unfulfilled. Prodigals allow little problems or needs to gain momentum. It can begin with any of the "Eight Trouble-Spots" and spawn a dissatisfaction or lack of fulfillment in the marriage. Whatever the "little fox" may be, if not addressed, it will definitely put the "vine" in great jeopardy (Song of Solomon 2:15).

Prodigal carelessly neglects to contain or curtail the growing restlessness in his or her heart. It may even be fed by fascinations, flirtations, or fantasies he or she plays in his or her mind. Fueling the fire may also be actions of neglect, abuse, criticism, or separation from his or her spouse. Distance can make the heart fonder or can make the emotional and physical disconnection more prevalent. Couples who must be apart for long periods can easily fall prey to this condition spawned by a form of separation anxiety or intimacy deprivation.

These are not excuses for betrayal that we seek. There are *no excuses* for adultery! There may be reasons why Prodigal is more susceptible to temptation than others, but there are no excuses for the actions of betrayal on his or her part. Seeking the motivations as to why something happened is not for the purpose of justifying the action. It is an attempt to understand the symptoms, setting, and the source eliciting his or her behavior.

When dealing with Prodigals in our counseling sessions, he or she has spoken of his or her vulnerability to adultery as a result of varying reasons. He or she has cited such reasons as: not feeling loved by a parent; needing more affection from his or her spouse; the spouse does not talk; spouse doesn't listen; spouse has no time for him or her; he or she feels unappreciated, mistreated, taken for granted, not complimented enough, sexually unfulfilled, bored, angry, frustrated; spouse does not understand his or her needs; experiencing a mid-life crisis; feels undesirable, unhappy, in a rut; or "it just happened."

It has been stated that there are four stages to a relationship. This is certainly true of the relationship of marriage. The first stage is the *forming* stage. The second is the stage called *storming*. This rocky period in the relationship should be followed by *norming*. The fourth stage is called *performing*.

Obviously, these stages, especially the *storming* stage, cannot be predicted like lunar phases but will be determined by the dynamics of the *three* personalities involved. The maturity and personality of the individuals conjoined with the collective persona of the couple will be the primary catalysts for creating a homeostatic relationship. It is a trio comprised of *him, her,* and *us* now shaping the dynamics of the marriage.

Movement through this storming stage was never reached by the first several generations of the Hatfields and the McCoys, so their fighting devolved into feuding of legendary proportions. The equilibrium of the norming and performing stages were never reached by these obstinate neighbors. As one noted couple stated, "We no longer have fights, just periodic moments of *intense* fellowship."

The transitions in these four stages are at the heart of the "you *two* shall become *one*" pronouncement. Since the development of a couple mentality is the ideal God had in mind, the Bible could literally say, "You two shall become a *third* element" in marriage. This would be the "us" stage of marital evolution.

You are not made one, but you can *become* one. Each person must decide if he or she is willing to forfeit some of his or her individuality in order to create the dynamic and dominant personality of the new unit. As is stated elsewhere in this book, the major hurdle in marriage is over the dilemma of deciding which *one* you will become. He always wants her to become a "mini me," and she desires the same of him. Any resistance in this area of adjusting simply extends the storming stage *ad finitum* until changes occur in the perspectives and conduct of the couple.

The Apostle Paul picks up on this theme in Ephesians 5:21, where he says, "Submitting yourselves one to another in the fear of God." While the word *submit* and its derivatives can elicit feelings of being abused, controlled, or some other negative connotation, the word really has a positive and significant effect on the harmony of the home.

The Greek word in Paul's text means to "subject, submit, or place yourself under" someone else as in the military ranking of personnel. A captain is not inferior to a major, but he is outranked and therefore *under* the major's command. The major may be an expert in aeronautics while the captain's expertise is weaponry. Rather than compete with one another, they compliment one another and utilize the collective knowledge and skill they each provide. This is called *synergism,* or "working together," and it is critical to a successful marriage.

A more practical and palatable application of the word "submit" means "to adjust" to one another. This concept is at the heart of all relationships. You must learn to adapt or adjust to the strengths, weaknesses, abilities, giftedness, knowledge, or skills of your partner or your spouse as part of the process for strengthening the bond between the concerned parties. Many couples want to enjoy this success but will not commit to the *process* for attaining it.

The safety of Paul's admonition is that submission here is a two-way street. Paul would go on to elaborate that wives should submit to their husbands, husbands to their wives, servants to their masters, and children to their parents, and all are to submit to the Lord. Submission means that you *adjust* to one another. You bend a little to accommodate the needs, desires, culture, or concerns of your spouse. Submission is not an enemy to marital accord, it is an ally.

The three keys to expediting this journey toward marital harmony are *commitment*, *communication*, and *conciliation*. If you are unwavering in your commitment to one another, there is a foundation upon which you can build a meaningful marriage. It you conjoin the willingness to "hear and be heard," you can communicate your views that will inform your spouse of your perspectives on these sensitive subjects of non-agreement.

Finally, you must develop the willingness to concede or

compromise in some areas. Unless it is the mountain you are willing to die on, you need to ask yourself if this is not another time when it is simply best to defer to the wishes or perspectives of your spouse.

Dr. Jay Adams has offered a very functional way of dealing with these *painful but predictable* choices we must make in life. This principle will work in all of your relationships, but it is especially helpful in both marriage and parenting. He describes the situations as "flame issues vs. swing issues."

Flame issues are highly combustible, dangerous, and potentially life- or relationship-threatening situations where immediate and decisive action must take place. A child playing near the road, reaching out to touch a hot stove, a spouse writing bad checks, physical abuse, or one who is driving under the influence of alcohol or drugs are simple examples that *may* demand the urgency of taking unilateral action without discussion or debate.

In addition, there can be somewhat less-urgent matters regarding intimacy, pornography, emotional abuse, or poor hygiene that are behaviors specific to one of the spouses that can ignite into a flame issue over time and repetition.

Swing issues get their name from realizing that, in the normal development of a child, he will sometimes get hurt while playing. You cannot refuse to allow your child to play simply because you know the chances exist that he may get a scrape or bruise at the playground. These are the painful but predictable "boo boos" that kids experience. We certainly would like to help them avoid them all, but we simply cannot.

In marriage, the challenges arise when the spouses cannot agree on which is a flame issue and which is a swing issue. What is a "swing" to one may be a "flame" to the other. Such mundane subjects as sports versus movies, butter versus margarine, fried or baked, earrings and purses (for the man), long hair versus short hair, beard or moustache, or a sports car versus an SUV can serve to cause friction in the relationship. These, and a host of other differences, can be seen by one as a simple, no big-deal swing issue, while the same situation may be concurrently viewed as a flame issue to be extinguished by the other.

The challenge for the couple is to define a process where they get to a common perspective or they simply learn when it is prudent to defer to the view of their partner. This is done by the aforementioned principles of commitment, communication, and conciliation.

The wise couple will realize that in the beginning of the relationship, there will be the evidence of many surprising and startling differences in perspectives that arise. These potential issues can seem to multiply faster than one can adjust. The important key to proper response is to remember that a forest is comprised of many trees, but to clear them you take it one tree at a time.

Do not try to tackle all the differences at once: It will definitely become hazardous to the marital and emotional health of the couple. Identify the *most* critical obstacle standing between you and your spouse and address it *only*. It isn't the shrub but the sequoia that is impeding the couple's progress toward unity. After you deal with that problem, move on to the less-stressful issues. Soon you will see that you have made significant inroads toward your common goal of a long and fulfilling marriage simply by advancing one tree (issue) at a time.

The next stage of *norming* comes as the "oneness" factor increases in the relationship. *Normal* is what you have established as the benchmarks of behavior that have been appropriately defined and embraced by the emerging couple. Normal certainly does not infer the spouses have individually and collectively attained perfection. Neither does it mean having the identical mores and manners as other couples. It is specific and personal to the individual couple.

Normal represents what has been etched out through the grid of trial and error, mistakes and forgiveness, or time and tolerance that brings a certain *sameness* to the couple's interaction. This allows the spouses to enjoy a "positive predictability" in their relationship, where they feel comfortable with the way they have decided to live their lives, respond to situations, and function as a family.

Normal is *linear* in that it is on a continuum with time. This may involve adjusting to such things as a change in spending habits, job status, health, mobility, mental proficiency, finances, in-laws, adult children, or grandchildren. Therefore, adjustments must constantly be made as new situations arise in the lives of the couple. Normal keeps evolving throughout the marriage.

The *performing* stage allows the couple to continue the journey of marriage feeling the safety of their spouse's shared sensibilities. Neither will try to rock the boat. Heated arguments have given way to thoughtful discussions. Each spouse has learned what to expect and what is expected. Each will place high value on harmony in the home and try to avoid doing anything that might shipwreck the marriage or bring distress to their companion. "Boring," you say? No, this is the blessing of *oneness*!

This final stage of performing is the closest to complete oneness the spouses will find. By the time they accomplish this level, they can be called the "Comfortable Couple." There is no time line for reaching this stage for a relaxed relationship. It is the product of the persistent pursuit of each spouse toward the shared vision of oneness for his or her marriage.

Someone shared an anonymous illustration with me about the spousal selection process. I am passing along now my amended version with the hope that it will give you insight into the capricious nature of the art of shopping for a spouse.

---

subject: the spouse store

A new matchmaking service has just opened in Atlanta, where a person may go to choose a companion. Among the instructions at the entrance is a description of how the store operates. You may visit the store *only once*!

There are six floors, and the attributes of the men and women increase as the shopper ascends the flights. There is, however, a catch... You may choose any spouse from a particular floor, or you may choose to go up a floor, but you cannot go back down except to exit the building! So a lonely person decides to go to the Spouse Store to find their ideal companion.

On the first floor, the sign on the door reads: Floor 1 - These men and women have jobs and love the Lord.

The second floor sign reads: Floor 2 - These men and women have jobs, love the Lord, and love kids.

The third floor sign reads: Floor 3 - These men and women have jobs, love the Lord, love kids, and are extremely good looking.

Wow, the shopper thinks, but feels compelled to keep going.

The person goes to the fourth floor and sign reads: Floor 4 - These men and women have jobs, love the Lord, love kids, are drop-dead good looking, and help with the housework.

"Oh, mercy me!" they exclaim. "I can hardly stand it!" Still, the shopper goes to the fifth floor and sign reads: Floor

5 - These men and women have jobs, love the Lord, love kids, are drop-dead gorgeous, help with the housework, and have a strong romantic streak.

The shopper is so tempted to stay but, after several minutes goes on to the sixth floor and the sign reads: Floor 6 - You are visitor 4,363,012 to this floor. There are no men or women on this floor. This floor exists solely as proof that shoppers who are expecting to find perfection in someone else are impossible to please and always want more.

Thank you for shopping at the Spouse Store. Watch your step as you exit the building, and have a nice, *realistic* day!

The interesting contrast that arises when involved in conjoint counseling is the perspective of the couple regarding the performing stage of the marriage. The unhappy spouse will boldly declare that his or her marriage is in a "rut." The other will retort that he or she thinks they are in a "groove." Ruts and grooves are at the heart of many marital conflicts. "What is the difference?" you might ask. It is a matter of perspective. What is a groove for one may be a rut for the other. For one, life is a routine that is *comfortable*. For the other, life is a routine that is *boring*. The difference lies in the eyes of the beholder.

The problems with Prodigal are exacerbated because he or she does not want to wait any longer for a personal or emotional need or desire to be fulfilled. There is emptiness and an acute sense of dissatisfaction about his or her life. The more Prodigal focuses on the thorns, the less he or she appreciates any of the roses in his or her life. Prodigal believes that time is running out, and he or she wants his or her "fair share" *now*. He or she does not believe that things will change in the foreseeable future. He or she seeks relief and pleasure and begins to require that something happen to satisfy his or her void.

While we are not justifying any rationalizations that Prodigal may use, we are also not minimizing any problems he or she may be experiencing. Be advised, Betrayed may or may not bear a very significant culpability in the conditions leading up to adultery. Numerous times, I have heard Betrayed lament his or her failure to understand the dynamics that were at work in his or her marriage. Many have admitted to ignorantly contributing to the susceptibility of his or her spouse to temptation. Our purpose is neither to blame Prodigal nor condone Betrayed but to help provide a way to recover from the events that have transpired in his or her marriage.

It must be understood that in some cases of adultery, Betrayed may bear no blame for the actions of Prodigal. As you read the New Testament account, which serves as our foundation, you will see that there is *no evidence* of a pre-existing relationship problem between the prodigal son and his father or his brother. You could conclude, from the omission of any reference to the contrary, that neither the father nor the older brother bore any responsibility for Prodigal's sudden exodus from the family and decision to engage in the tawdry conduct of the far country citizenry.

The implications drawn from the Luke text are that both the father and the older brother were caught off guard by Prodigal's decision. The prodigal's demand for his share (approximately one-third) of the estate was an insult to the father. He was saying to his father, "I can't sit around and wait for you to die. I want my share now!" It was not the father's fault that he was in good health and might live for years to come. Therefore, we must also conclude that there will be occasions of marital infidelity where no fault can be ascribed to the betrayed spouse, and Betrayed needs to accept this fact.

3

rebellion

"…Took his journey into a far country" (Luke 15:13).

The text now tells us that the prodigal son liquidated everything he inherited and left home with his stash of cash. He was soon to be separated from it by his squandering, wasteful, and wanton way of living.

This author will now apprise you, the readers, of the following disclaimer: I shall periodically interject into this body of work truisms, aphorisms, and insights affectionately called "Frazierisms." They are statements that I'm not sure if I coined or not, but they have become such a part of me that I claim them for my own with no disservice intended should there be an unknown author.

The first Frazierism is, "Most people do not mind suffering in silence as long as *everyone knows they are.*" Suffering is *not* like solitaire: no one wants to experience it alone. The human soul yearns for compassion and companionship during our travails. This is nowhere more evident than when a marriage begins to deteriorate. You may find this referenced other times in this book, but it is a powerful insight for us to consider. This dynamic statement comes to us via the song "The Birth of the Blues." The composers, B.G. DeSylva, Ray Henderson, and Lew Brown, wrote,

> "And then they nursed it,
> Rehearsed it, And gave out the news,
> That the Southland gave birth to the blues!"

If you want the formula for dissatisfaction, dysphoria, dysthymia, dysteliology, and divorce, you need look no farther. When you begin the anthems of anguish in your heart and then share them with others, it is just a matter of time until your feelings of frustration will follow. After all, the number one cause of divorce is unforgiveness. When a spouse refuses to forgive a trespass, the stockpiling of pain and frustration begins. Drastic steps may not be far away.

The Prodigal now begins thinking of a way to escape. This starts with a search for a new identity, new friends, and a new environment. He or she no longer believes he or she can find what he or she wants or needs at home. Prodigal thinks a change of scenery will help. From Prodigal's point of view, the *groove* of their marriage has morphed into a *rut* with no end in sight.

The yearning for a "far country" becomes more and more of an obsession. Prodigal begins to explore different places with different associates. This initiates the development of a secret life apart from his or her spouse. He or she does not fully realize that the world is drawing him or her away from his or her home. Consequently, Prodigal does not resist the allure of the world. He or she may not be in rebellion yet, but it can be seen from where he or she is now standing.

This "far country" allurement is insidious because it offers boundary-free living. The contrast between fidelity and infidelity is seen quite vividly in a statement by Christ in Matthew 7:13–14. He says, "Enter ye in at the strait gate: for wide *is* the gate, and broad *is* the way, that leadeth to destruction, and many there be which go in thereat: Because strait *is* the gate, and narrow is the way, which leadeth unto life, and few there be that find it."

According to Ralph Earle, in his work *Word Meanings in the New Testament*, "The Greek word for 'strait' simply refers to the narrow door of self-denial." By comparison, the word for "broad" is actually a compound word meaning "broad country." Earle says,

> This word by our Lord and only used here in the New Testament suggests a "wide-open country with no fences and no boundaries." In other words, there are no rules, regulations or restrictions placed upon the inhabitants so one may do just as he pleases. One may go anywhere he wants and live as undisciplined life as he chooses. He need not worry about getting off the road. He can't [*sic*].

Still another distinction should be noted to comprehend the full import of Christ's teaching. In verse 14, a different word for "narrow" is used. This one is much more specific than that used in the former verse. This word in Greek means "to press, compress, restrict, or confine." Now according to Earle, this means, "Only those who are willing to live godly lives in an ungodly world, to be holy in heart and life, can find their way *home* to heaven (emphasis mine)."

Christ is teaching that there are two worlds, and these two worlds are indeed bi-polar. They are utter extremes or diametrically opposed to one another. One leads to conformity with Kingdom principles and values. The other is a "wide-open spaces" lifestyle governed only by one's imagination and volition. The great warning that all prodigals need to hear is that your volition can lead you to becoming violated. There is a pecking order in "far country," and your choices can be trumped by the coercion of another. Since there are no boundaries to restrict your behavior, there are also no fences to protect you from others.

The rebellion of Prodigal includes adopting different mindsets, values, and perspectives from this "far country." At the same time he or she is rethinking his or her marriage vows, he or she begins to rebel against his or her Christian values and pursuits. Down deep he or she probably still loves God very much. However, a major crisis looms closer and closer on the horizon: "Do I stay and suffer, or do I leave and *hope* for a better life?" After nursing his or her unhappiness and rehearsing it repeatedly in his or her mind, he or she finally "gives out the news."

Someone is always there when you are ready to vent your frustrations. The devil sees to it that you will have a "Job's comforter" within earshot. We are not talking about a bedspread or a blanket when we say comforter. We are talking about someone strategically planted by the enemy of marriage. He or she will have just the words for Prodigal that will reassure him or her that he or she has every right to ditch this marriage and look for sweeter nectar in another field.

Enough people have shared in the same misery Prodigal is experiencing to convince him or her to "jump ship" and look for his or her *real* soulmate. After all, they say, "If this marriage were right, you would not feel so wronged." The seeds of rebellion are beginning to germinate, and Prodigal can now more easily imagine making a break for it. Just then, the classic country song might come wafting over the radio entitled "It Don't Feel like Sinning to Me," and Prodigal feels he or she has received his or her confirmation to "cut and run."

Rebellion seldom produces the soundest of judgment or decisions normally based on due diligence. It is usually accompanied by impulsive and foolish actions that may seem totally out of character for the person. However, Prodigal is no longer that same person he or she once was, and many things will change before the final chapter is written on his or her rebellion.

4

recklessness

"…Wasted his substance with riotous living" (Luke 15:13).

Simultaneous with the appearance of "Rebellion" is its conjoined twin, "Reckless." When the Scripture warns in Numbers 32:23, "Behold, ye have sinned against the LORD: and be sure your sin will find you out," God is not offering an idle threat. He is exhorting all Prodigals, of every description, to consider his or her actions before he or she takes an ill-advised action.

Ill-conceived plans precede ill-conceived actions, and this reckless behavior will often produce fatal results. This is why God so graciously heralds His warning to Prodigal that the outcome of his or her recklessness may yield a harvest of incalculable sorrow that he or she may be unable to bear.

Unfortunately, Prodigal is tired of what he or she considers wasting precious time on an ill-fated marriage. He or she is becoming more and more convinced that the time is ripe to live it up. You may have heard this commercial before, "You only go around once in this world, so get all the *gusto* you can get." Prodigal may not know exactly what "gusto" means, but if it means excitement, thrills, pleasure, or passion, you can count him or her in. He or she certainly does not feel he or she has that now.

The problem with the gusto the world offers Prodigal is what he or she has to do to get it. It isn't found neatly packaged in a family picnic setting, at a church function, or by a child's bedside. That constitutes "domestic gusto," and it comes hermetically sealed in the wrapper of godly relationships built on a foundation of love and trust. Domestic gusto leaves no guilty conscience, no bad aftertaste, and no lingering fears of exploitation and exposure.

The problem with domestic gusto is that it is difficult to market because of what appears to be such a small target audience. Who gets excited about normalcy and respectability anymore? Who orders a big case of "same ole, same ole" when you can drink a different flavor any time you wish? Remember, it was Howard Johnson Hotels that set the benchmark for ice cream with its twenty-eight flavors. So, according to an old George Jones/Tammy Wynette ballad, how do you entice the "jet set" to revert to being the "Chev-ro-let set"? People in the fast lane of this world's social and moral permissiveness do not quickly respond to the marketing strategies for things like monogamy, marriage morality, holiness, or sanctity.

Satan, however, is a master marketer. He and his imps know exactly how to sell the sizzle to the Prodigal who feels his or her life has fizzled. They use "hot-button" words like *thrill, free, variety, inclusive, nonjudgmental, consenting adults*, and a host of others to entice the waffling one to take a bite from their big apple. The Christian life seems dull[2] compared to the glitter and glamour promised the Prodigal if he or she would just take the lover's leap.

What most Prodigals plan next is to use what they *have* so they can get what they *want*. To do this, he or she says "goodbye" to the domestic gusto and "hello" to the bootleg. Prodigal can be sure that there are moonshiners at every turn just waiting to give him or her a taste of his or her newest batch of "rot gut." And that is exactly what this counterfeit life will become with regular consumption: a major pain that will not go away and can ultimately destroy him or her from the inside. Prodigal is about to make the decision that will have a colossal impact on him or her and his or her family forever!

To make the switch from the domestic to the bootleg, Prodigal has to change the scenery and try to get the taste of the domestic out of his or her mouth. Prodigal does not want to be reminded of vows, restraints, expectations, and convictions. That old taste has to go and a new taste cultivated for the palate. He or she pushes beyond the parameters that his or her marriage established.

Prodigal now starts taking risks with temptation. He or she allows fantasies and flirtations to occupy his or her mind. Things that were formerly "out of bounds" now seem acceptable. He or she likes the tingle of these illicit thoughts. Prodigal is getting more and more comfortable with the "daydreams about night-things" and of finding happiness elsewhere. His or her new motto becomes "Home is where the heart *was*!"

Prodigal decides it's time to live a little and gradually lowers his or her guard against adultery. Prodigal's mind tells him or her to try a new partner if he or she wishes. There are always the advances of the bootleggers on the corner, in his or her office, or in his or her neighborhood, to whom he or she can submit. After all, he or she says it is his or her body, and he or she will not get caught if he or she is careful.

That is the popular rationale of the pathetically deceived. Bootleg gusto is about to make a sale, and Prodigal is the unwitting client. He or she is getting ready to sell his or her marriage for "a bowl of pottage" (Genesis 25:29–34).

5

rummaging

"A famine in the land and he began to be in want." Luke 15:14

The parable tells that the prodigal son spent everything he had wastefully. He became completely depleted of funds and was desperate for someone to intervene on his behalf.

Just as Esau despised what he had done when he sold his birthright for a hot meal, so Prodigal is on a collision course with a harsh reality. With this growing sense of emptiness and unfulfillment, a greater distance is developing between spouses. There is a void that Prodigal cannot seem to fill. He or she is increasingly sure that his or her spouse simply does not understand his or her special needs. Worse yet is when Prodigal believes he or she understands but does not seem to care.

Prodigal may begin to feel less and less appreciated and approved by his or her spouse, even though he or she may not, as yet, have committed an overt act of adultery. The feelings of emptiness, loneliness, abandonment, and depression become constant companions. Prodigal desperately wants *someone* who will make him or her feel alive and happy again.

He or she is searching for a spark to life that will fill the gaping hole in his or her heart. Those feelings set in motion either a conscious or subconscious desire to rummage his or her surroundings and find the person who will give him or her the satisfaction he or she craves.

The problem with rummaging is that you may not know exactly what you want or where to find it. Rummaging represents a sense of futility and frustration brought on by a keen sense of loss or deprivation. Prodigal must now go "dumpster diving" in hopes that he or she will find something of value amid all the refuse. He or she hopes to beat all the odds and find a "jewel in a junkyard."

This phase in the Prodigal's life may be a mental exercise of exploring all available options. There is still time to salvage the marriage because irreparable harm may not have occurred. But the more rummaging, the more likely an overt act of infidelity will soon occur. When a person becomes hungry, he or she starts looking for food anywhere he or she can find it, and sanitation is the least of his or her concerns. What is found in the dumpster may taste good to the palate, but it may be poison to the person.

Prodigal feels the increasing pangs of the emotional famine in his or her land. As he or she evaluates his or her marriage, he or she sees no green pastures, just barren fields where love once grew. He or she may start rummaging on the Internet, at work, at church, with neighbors, at a bar or at a brothel. Prodigal thinks he or she will get lucky and discover a diamond in a "dime store." He or she pokes around anywhere he or she can in hopes that he or she will find the perfect person to meet his or her needs. He or she is looking for a love feast that will satisfy his or her famine.

Prodigal will soon discover you never discover fine dining in a dumpster.

6

rendezvous

"He joined himself to a citizen of that country." Luke 15:15

When Prodigal starts looking for a new soulmate, partner, or lover, he or she will eventually find one in the world outside of his or her marriage. Satan has more than enough people who are willing to accommodate his or her desire for the illicit. They will gladly lead Prodigal into immorality and adultery. The lover will encourage Prodigal to betray his or her trusting spouse and begin an affair with him or her.

At first, it all seems so innocent and exciting. This illicit partner can make Prodigal *feel* so special, so loved, so accepted, and so alive. He or she can arrange special meeting times and places that stimulate the basic erotic and sensual nature of Prodigal. He or she knows all the locations that lead to provocative, fulfilling, emotional, and sexual encounters. After all, he or she may be an *old resident* of this new, far country where Prodigal has taken his or her journey. The new lover knows all the back roads where they can lead Prodigal astray.

Prodigal is in carnal country now, and adultery is the

national pastime. This "far country" is not measured in physical distance but in emotional and spiritual disconnection from their home and their mate. Many prodigals never leave his or her residence, but he or she forsakes the sexual exclusivity of his or her home. The detachment is real whether he or she actually moves out of his or her house or not. He or she may still see family and friends, may still sleep in the same bed as his or her spouse, but internally and emotionally Prodigal has pulled the plug on monogamy.

"Bootleg gusto" is served on tap in this far country. Citizens here have learned all the trappings of the "Lifestyle of the Illicit and Repulsive." The Lover knows the language, the proper attire, the familiar hangouts, and the players in the game. He or she sees Prodigal's naiveté, and gladly offers the friendly tour of the social and sexual scene. Prodigal will soon see that this is a country that truly "eats up its inhabitants" (Numbers 13:32).

Though Prodigal does not realize it now, the aliens will soon pounce on him or her with a ferocity that he or she has never witnessed. Prodigal does not know just how wicked his or her new playmates can be. After all, the king of this far country is none other than Satan himself. He sets the rules for his subjects, and they blindly follow his lead. Prodigal has made an enormous error in judgment by aligning himself or herself with a renegade band of marriage marauders.

There are no warning labels on bootleg gusto. Prodigal is never advised to consult a professional before indulging. The moonshiners want everyone to become hooked on their illicit brew. No one in this far country will advise Prodigal to be careful, exercise caution, or use moderation. This country is known for its lack of restraint. If Satan doesn't wear a seatbelt, why should his subjects? This is "live and let live country."

Prodigal is not prepared for this reckless attitude but gradually adapts to the promiscuous life that is prevalent here.

Prodigal eventually gets over being a *tourist* and starts to feel at home with the new life in the far country. He or she has now or will soon cross the line and engage in the sin of adultery. This new country may be far from family, friends, God, spouse, vows, and self-respect, but it is *not* far from a crisis that is about to rock Prodigal's world.

7

repulsion

"…Feeding swine." Luke 15:15

The illicit partner's ultimate goal is to have Prodigal feed his or her "swine" (doing that which is an abomination to God and a violation of the marriage vows). He or she can sink no lower, fall no farther, debase and degrade himself or herself no more than to commit adultery. According to the Bible, the breaking of the Seventh Commandment is the only one that carries a *self-inflicted penalty* clause. Prodigal is now willfully sinning and participating in actions that are morally and spiritually reprehensible.

The Bible says in Proverbs 9:17–18, "Stolen waters are sweet, and bread eaten in secret is pleasant. But he knoweth not that the dead are there; and that her guests are in the depths of hell." King Solomon would graphically describe the essence of the far country lifestyle. He used the words "stolen, secret, dead, and hell" to counteract the slick marketing done by the "Far Country Chamber of Commerce" in its recruitment of Prodigal. The king's graphic warning is pivotal for those being influenced to set sail for the far country.

Prodigal is now "joined" (literally, "to be glued together") to a citizen of the world and is becoming the servant of sin. First Corinthians 6:16 states, "What? Know ye not that he which is joined to an harlot is one body? for two, saith he, shall be one flesh." God considers a sexual union an extremely serious matter. Whether the "harlot" is male or female, the verdict is the same: Prodigals *can never* undo the spiritual, physical, and emotional damage done when he or she engages in illicit sexual relations.

Something metaphysical transpires during intimacy, and the Prodigal and his or her lover become "one body." If this infidelity were not a serious offense against God, Betrayed, his or her family, and himself or herself, Paul would have never been inspired to warn all potential Prodigals about its severity. Just as you can never "un-ring a bell," adultery is a deed you can never undo!

Prodigal now has a new lover and must submit to his or her new partner, who has wishes and demands for his or her time, energy, emotions, and body. Thankfully, as time goes by, Prodigal cannot ignore the feelings of repulsion, regret, loss of respect, and exploitation that begin to surface after he or she has been assigned "swine duty." The whole swine scene begins to stink more and more with each passing day. The flirtatious has become the filthy, the romantic has become the rancid, and the sexy has become a stench, which is nauseating to Prodigal.

Here Prodigal stands, feeding corn to the swine while he or she tries to survive off the husks. Husks and shucks were not on the menu when the "Bootleg" peddler came calling. It was never mentioned that, in a brief period, Prodigal would be relegated to the roll of a slave with the swine dining better than him or her. How far Prodigal has fallen in this far country. His or her lover's tender "sweet nothings" whispered in a moment of passion have been replaced by the constant cacophonic squealing and snorting of stinking, filthy, gluttonous swine.

Everything about the trough, pigs, pen, slop, mud, manure, hogs, corn, husks, cobs, shucks, even bacon, sausage, and ham are now a disgusting thought for Prodigal. The stench and the stigma are becoming more than Prodigal can bear. It is nearly impossible to look the lover or the "lard factory" in the eyes without feeling repulsion about his or her behavior and how far he or she has fallen into sin. Every snort and squeal seems to be saying, "Go home. Go home. Go home where you belong."

Somewhere in my educational process, I discovered the following list by an anonymous writer. It appropriately addressed ten simple, yet successful ways to avoid the sin of adultery. I have added a little of my own perspectives in its presentation.

1. Do not do or say anything you would not do or say in the presence of your spouse.

2. Avoid work-related meetings with a member of the opposite sex outside the workplace.

3. Do not drink alcohol with a member of the opposite sex.

4. Avoid allowing your marriage to become monotonous. Keep adding spontaneity and spice to your relationship.

5. Make time for yourselves as a couple where you are not with family, friends, or kids. Keep dating alive in your marriage.

6. Nip problems in the bud before they blossom into something more serious.

7. Take time for yourself where you can relax, read, refresh, or reinvigorate your spirit, mind, and body.

8. Attempt to make periodic "I love you" contacts with your spouse several times each day. This can be an e-mail, a card, a note placed in his or her jacket or purse, or a quick phone call to simply remind your spouse that they are loved by you.

9. Stay *actively* engaged and involved in the relationship. Marriage is no place to coast or become complacent and lazy. It is good to ask your spouse periodically how the relationship is going or if there is something that you need to work on to improve the marriage.

10. Avoid personal, non-work-related contact with anyone you are inappropriately attracted to or someone who seems to be attracted to you. Period. No exceptions!

Because adultery always has been and always will be a sin, be advised that it contains the elements for spiritual and emotional decomposition for the participants. Just as it takes time to make sewage, it may take some time for the adultery to abscess. However, be assured it will!

The spiritual stench from violating God's mandate of fidelity will eventually begin to surface, and you, just like Prodigal, will experience the toxicity and effluvium of your sin.

8

remorse

"No man gave unto him." Luke 15:16

Guilt and grief, sorrow and shame accompany Prodigal each day as he or she brings the swill to the pigpen. The passion of the new soulmate has been obscured with these porcine portraits of a life now near shambles. Maybe the new lover no longer wants Prodigal. Perhaps Prodigal has become disillusioned and discovers that a new lover is not the answer after all. Whatever the motivation, Prodigal now lives with a foreboding sense of regret about the decision to move to the far country and take up with a *pig farmer*.

The enigmatic thing is, Prodigal never suspected his or her new life would end up "hanging with the hogs." There was certainly no mention of that during those first illicit interludes the new lover and he or she enjoyed together. The new lover never reeked of "pig patties" when he or she began his or her tryst. Never once did new lover order pork chops or a BLT sandwich when they went out to eat. Who would have guessed that lurking behind that intoxicating personality and seductive smile beat the heart of a hog lover?

Mental motion pictures of better times and safer situations run frame by frame through Prodigal's mind. The projector seems to be on "auto-run." Every frame brings back painful memories of a life left behind. Innocence is gone, trust is shattered, virtue is tainted, and reputation is ruined all because of the reckless and rebellious acts of immorality. Prodigal's sadness is overwhelming, and his or her misery is all but unbearable.

Prodigal's daily fare has been the tedium of handling the husks. But now he or she cannot eat. The guts wrench; the heart aches with condemnation and guilt. Prodigal's spirit has withered, and no one in the new country really seems to care whether he or she survives. As long as Prodigal keeps feeding the swine, the citizens of this far country will use him or her for their own gratification. After they have used Prodigal and abused him or her, they will discard Prodigal just as hogs do the husks.

Citizens of the far country cannot satisfy Prodigal's anguish. They cannot comfort him or her or pray with him or her. Prodigal will *never* find what he or she is searching for in this far country. Prodigal longs for peace and purity. Oh, how Prodigal wishes he or she had stayed in the comfort of "Father's house." He or she wishes that he or she had never met the other person, had never let himself or herself sink so low, had never betrayed his or her God, his or her spouse, his or her family and friends.

"If only I could be pure again. If only ... "

The grief that Prodigal feels is normal for anyone who has experienced a significant loss in life. Whether the loss is in the realm of marriage, finances, health, employment, family, or the death of a loved one, the potential impact is the same. To facilitate the healing process, psychologists have identified what they call the "Five Stages of the Grief Reaction."

Since both Prodigal and Betrayed have lost something very significant, they are both having to deal with enormous feelings of grief.

The Five Stages of the Grief Reaction are as follows:

1. *Denial.* "No! It can't be!" is the universal and primal scream of bad news. Upon hearing of a significant loss, the majority of people will go into a self-defense posture of denying that it could be true by crying, "This cannot be happening to me!"

2. *Anger Turned Outward.* At some point, after the initial shock and denial, comes the desire to place blame on someone for your pain. Your hostility and anger may be directed toward the drunk driver, the assailant, your spouse, the neighbor, the mortgage company, your new boss, the banker, stockbroker, or whomever you believe is culpable for your loss. This is the stage that allows you to blame someone else for your loss.

3. *Anger Turned Inward.* It is at this point that the indicting finger gets pointed toward us *by us.* Being the self-deprecating people that most are, it is not long until you begin feeling that you should shoulder the blame for the tragedy. Expressions like, "If I had only been there," "If I had only checked on them more," "If I had just read the small print," "If I had just seen it coming," "If I...." You can fill in the blank a hundred times when you start to blame yourself for the loss. You may have had some responsibility in the situation that led to the loss, but for your ultimate healing, you must move on to the next stage of the grief reaction.

4. *True Grief.* This is the stage that each person must reach as quickly as possible. If you get mired in one of the former stages, you will never *actually* grieve your loss. True grief comes when you allow yourself the freedom to express your feelings of loss and pain. The Bible says, "Joseph wept at the death of his father." In the New Testament, it states that "Jesus wept" at the tomb of his friend Lazarus. Weeping does wonders for the grieving soul.

The final stage of grief reaction is

5. *Resolution.* This is the ultimate goal for the grieving person. You *must* reach the place where you can say to yourself that life goes on in spite of the crushing circumstances. You didn't die when your marriage, job, parent, child, spouse, or relationship died. You cannot allow what you lost to destroy *you*. You must accept your loss, express your grief, and, with God's help, move forward. You need to reach the place where you decide that you will not allow what died in your life to kill you. This is "resolution," and it works for Prodigal and it works for Betrayed. Try it the next time you get hit with bad news. These five stages lead you on the road to emotional recovery.

9

recognition

"He came to himself." Luke 15:17

Prodigal is finally coming to his or her senses. His or her lover does not look so enticing anymore. The meeting places no longer hold their mystique. The titillating rendezvous no longer appeal to his or her emotions. The tingle is replaced by a tangled web of regret and self-loathing.

Prodigal has discovered that there is no future in this "far country." After all, if the illicit partner will cheat *with* him or her, he or she will cheat *on* him or her. Prodigal remembers that he or she was created for fellowship with God and his or her family. There is someone back home who loves him or her and may still be committed to him or her. He or she feels lonely and wishes he or she could go back to the safety and sanctity of the home, back to the marriage and family he or she has forsaken by adulterous behavior.

Prodigal knows in his or her heart that he or she does not fit in this lifestyle. He or she is unhappier now than before the adultery because he or she has sinned against God and Betrayed. Prodigal has discovered firsthand that you cannot drink stolen waters and not suffer severe consequences. That which recently looked so refreshing, enticing, and intoxicating has proven to be a polluted cesspool of contamination.

Prodigal has finally come to his or her senses and decides to forsake this illicit relationship and reunite, if possible, with Betrayed. If the adultery is undisclosed, perhaps Betrayed will never know Prodigal has "been away" and joined himself or herself to an illicit partner. If Betrayed knows about the adultery, there is some serious repair work ahead for the couple in order to discover if it is possible to restore the marriage.

How long does it take for an adulterer to reach this decision? No one knows the answer to that question. There is simply no time limit on prodigality. The biblical account does not tell us the time frame it took for the wayward son to hit rock bottom and return home. It tells us he went out full and came back empty, but no one is sure how long the process took.

This timing variable is the constant companion in Betrayed's mind. The question of "how long?" keeps resonating in his or her heart. Sadly, no one can tell him or her when Prodigal will get his or her fill of the husks and want to come home. Betrayed's daily prayer is for Prodigal to have an epiphany of sorts and recognize that home is where the heart *wants* to be.

10

rehearsal

"He said…" Luke 15:17

Preparing for the greatest "*mea culpa*" of our life is difficult for anyone. The admission of our own culpability and guilt is almost universally met with enormous resistance. We just do not want to admit our mistakes or failures. It is so much easier and far more painless to shift the blame to someone else. That attitude has become a normal way of life…just blame the other person!

The defense mechanism of blame shifting had its origin in the Garden of Eden with the world's first couple. There were only four voices on earth at this time, and the day something horrible happened the *blame games* began. You remember how the serpent persuaded Eve to eat the forbidden fruit and she then coaxed Adam to take a bite. When God confronted Adam and Eve (actually, God named them both Adam because He saw them as *one*. Adam later changed her name to Eve) about their sin, she said it was the serpent that was to blame.

When Adam was confronted, he said it was God's fault

because of the weak wife He had been given. It is always the way of least resistance to lay the blame on someone else when we refuse to accept accountability for our own errors and omissions. God, correctly, said it was Adam who was to blame for this calamity. Blame shifting has been with us since that day when our Federal head, Adam, tried to lay the blame for his sin on God. People still resort to that absurd and foolish tactic today.

In actuality, it was Adam who was solely responsible for the terrible sin of his wife and himself. When you read the Genesis account of Creation, you discover that God formed man from the dust of the ground *outside* the Garden of Eden (Genesis 2:7). Verse 8 continues by describing God planting the Garden and the placing of the man inside Eden. Man was not made from the dust inside of Eden but outside, and he was brought in and given dominion by God's invitation. There was *no woman* on the scene at this time.

Genesis 2:16–17 states, "And the LORD God commanded the *man*, saying, Of every tree of the garden thou mayest freely eat: But of the tree of the knowledge of good and evil, thou shalt not eat of it: for in the day that thou eatest thereof thou shalt surely die." This was God speaking only to Adam since Eve would not be made until later in this chapter.

This chronology brings us to a critical point of understanding how the serpent could *deceive* Eve and not Adam. It is because Eve *never* heard God's prohibition against eating the fruit from the forbidden tree and therefore had no basis for disputing this temptation from Satan. She was not present when God spoke to Adam. Her only way of being warned was through the intervention of Adam. Knowledge would have been her vanguard against deception. One cannot be deceived when they *know*. Obviously, Adam failed to properly inform Eve about the only rule God gave for Garden living.

God had placed Adam in charge of the Garden and all of its contents. He clearly neglected to do an adequate job of instructing his new wife as to the urgency of using their *serpent repellant*, which was and still is, "Thus saith the Lord." Adam's neglect left Eve vulnerable to the wiles of the devil, and consequently Satan's deception led her to sin.

Women have borne the blame for the fall of man far too long. Since God clearly says Eve was fooled and Adam wasn't, it is evident that Adam knew the truth but was irresponsible in not preparing his wife to handle temptation. God did not exonerate Eve for her sin, but he did establish that Adam bore a higher level of accountability for this treeside tragedy. The verdict was not that Eve was such a poor wife, but Adam was a careless husband (See 2 Corinthians 11:3 and 1 Timothy 2:13).

Perhaps being remiss in his connubial duty was caused by Adam's excitement over God bringing him a gorgeous, naked woman to play with. If he was like his eventual male progeny, he probably was replaying the statements God made about Eve, like "bone of my bone and flesh of my flesh" and "naked, cleaving, clinging and *she* has no hang-ups or inhibitions" (Genesis 2:22–25). This may have caused Adam to forget to minister God's word of warning to his beautiful, sensual, and susceptible wife. Many wives will concur that it seems their husband has only *one* thing on his mind. Consequently, Adam's neglect brought the entrance of sin and their exit from the Garden of Eden.

Returning to our account, we see that as much as Prodigal might like to blame Betrayed for the conditions and events that prompted the betrayal, he or she knows that the final decision to betray was his or hers. The magnitude of this sin means this is no "oops, I goofed" kind of apology that Prodigal must give. The level of pain and anguish caused by Prodigal and suffered by Betrayed escalates these acts of admission and contrition to the apex on the repentance scale. Prodigal cannot just "wing it" and somehow hope he or she will say the right things to make amends. There must be very careful wording of *what* was done and *why* it was done if Betrayed is going to take this repentance seriously.

Prodigal plays his or her words repeatedly in his or her mind while deciding just the right things to say. Explaining the betrayal will be the hardest thing he or she has ever or will ever do in his or her life. How can he or she apologize for the infidelity and the unimaginable grief that he or she has caused Betrayed? The offender may even decide it best to write down what he or she wants to say to the offended so there will be no oversights or omissions.

A major concern for Prodigal is how will he or she convince Betrayed of his or her sorrow. As a deceiver who blindsided his or her companion with this infidelity, he or she cannot just assume that Betrayed will believe he or she is speaking the whole truth. God's axiom proves that seeds of deception sown culminate in a harvest of distrust reaped. He says in Galatians 6:7–8, "Be not deceived; God is not mocked: for whatsoever a man soweth, that shall he also reap."

As Prodigal begins the emotional and physical journey home, he or she repeats and rehearses the words of disclosure and the unalleviated sorrow that he or she wants to convey to Betrayed. No matter how far the distance Prodigal has to travel, this is the longest trip of his or her life.

II

return

"I will arise and go…" Luke 15:18

The steps home are much more difficult than the departure. It can be easier to *step out* than *step back*. Prodigal's excitement regarding the return home is tempered by the anxiety of probable disclosure and possible retaliation by Betrayed. Prodigal has no idea what awaits him or her when he or she steps through the door of home and faces Betrayed with the facts.

Prodigal knows he or she has shattered trust, destroyed confidence, betrayed his or her spouse, and desecrated the vows of marriage. Returning is courageous, but it will not be easy. It is not a pleasant, idyllic, emotional time for Prodigal. He or she is fairly certain the return will be devastating to Betrayed when he or she hears that adultery has been committed. Perhaps in Betrayed's naiveté, he or she still wants to believe that the departure was only physical and emotional, not sexual.

Prodigal must be willing to initiate all the necessary steps for reuniting the marriage. Starting with the decision to return and the "self-talk" boosting his or her courage, the trip home is filled with trepidation of the highest magnitude. Very few "Betrayeds" accept infidelity graciously. Police reports are filled with acts of violence occurring after the disclosure of adultery. This does not escape Prodigal's mind.

The return trip provides the time for Prodigal to accept his or her responsibility. The attitude must be right if there is to be any chance that the outcome will be a reuniting of the couple. But what is the right attitude for Prodigal? It certainly does not include blaming Betrayed, gloating over the illicit escapades, or comparing Betrayed with the citizens of "far country."

Betrayed's attitude and responses are totally unpredictable, but Prodigal's must not be. Prodigal must be prepared for whatever reaction he or she receives. If Betrayed knows about the infidelity, his or her response will be affected by the depth of hurt and rejection he or she has experienced. If Betrayed did not know of the adultery, the response to hearing the shocking news may be much more severe. Since Prodigal may not know how much Betrayed knows, he or she must be prepared for anything.

Just as the prodigal son had no assurances of how his father would respond to his return, Prodigal may not know if there awaits a welcome mat or a closed door. The driving obsession in Prodigal's heart is to go home. If you can never be "at home" again, it is still better to be near home than in a far country.

Prodigal's decision and desires in returning home are summed up in these magnificent lyrics to the nineteenth-century hymn "Lord, I'm Coming Home," by William J. Kirkpatrick (1838–1921).

1. I've wandered far away from God,
   Now I'm coming home,
   The paths of sin too long I've trod,
   Lord, I'm coming home.

2. I've wasted many precious years,
   Now I'm coming home;
   I now repent with bitter tears,
   Lord, I'm coming home.

3. I've tired of sin and straying, Lord,
   Now I'm coming home;
   I'll trust Thy love,
   believe Thy word,
   Lord, I'm coming home.

4. My soul is sick my heart is sore,
   Now I'm coming home;
   My strength renew,
   my hope restore,
   Lord, I'm coming home.

Chorus:
   Coming home,
   coming home,
   Never-more to roam,
   Open wide Thine arms of love,
   Lord, I'm coming home.

repentance

"I have sinned..." Luke 15:19

The prodigal's contrition and confession can open the door for deliverance for him or her and healing for his or her spouse. The prodigal must admit that he or she did not just "goof up." Prodigal *sinned*! Really sinned. Badly sinned. Regarding marriage, he or she committed the most repulsive, degrading, devastating act his or her spouse can conceive. *Nothing hurts more, nor takes longer to heal, than betrayal by a spouse.*

Prodigal must remember that he or she has had time to process the adulterous actions and to sort through all the emotions before disclosing the betrayal to his or her spouse. True repentance must emanate from the heart. It must accept responsibility for the failure and never minimize the depths of anguish the adultery has caused. Real repentance means to have a total, radical change of mind about the infidelity. Prodigal must declare that his or her actions were sinful in the sight of God and the results devastating to

Betrayed. Therefore, his or her infidelity can never be justifiable behavior.

Change is never so much a *constant* as it is in marriage. There are changes required to eliminate poor attitudes and behaviors. Conversely, there are changes needed to promote better harmony in the home. When do most people get willing to make changes? When the pain and discomfort of remaining status quo exceeds the perceived painful processes required for change.

In psychology there is a tandem of terminologies utilized for change appropriately called "dehabituation and rehabituation." These terms refer to the cessation of an old habit and the introduction of an alternative habit. You replace a bad or undesirable habit with a new, better habit. There is no vacuum when something is removed and something else is brought in to take its place. The complete process involves removing and replacing behavioral dynamics.

This method for change has its origin, not in the behavioral sciences, but in the Word of God. The Apostle Paul states in Ephesians 4:22–24, "That ye *put off* concerning the former conversation the old man, which is corrupt according to the deceitful lusts; And be renewed in the spirit of your mind; And that ye *put on* the new man, which after God is created in righteousness and true holiness" (emphases mine). This is first-century dehabituation and rehabituation defined and described!

Paul once more refers to this dynamic of change as he writes in Colossians 3: 8–10, "But now ye also *put off* all these; anger, wrath, malice, blasphemy, filthy communication out of your mouth. Lie not one to another, seeing that ye have put off the old man with his deeds; And have *put on* the new man, which is renewed in knowledge after the image of him that created him" (emphases mine).

This again is a description of first-century dehabituation and rehabituation. Paul was dealing with changes that God required in His children. Thankfully, He did not leave the subject of optional or alternative behaviors open to discussion. Paul says the liar must make a decision to stop deceiving and tell the truth, the thief must decide to stop stealing and go to work, the angry must stop expressing wrath or rage and start showing love, and the vile must stop speaking filth and incorporate wholesome words in their speech.

These are just a few of the "put offs and put on" directly from God Himself. While there are many other behavioral contrasts in the Bible, the one we are most concerned with is that the adulterous person must put off the activities of infidelity and put on the conduct of chastity and faithfulness.

The words from the Scripture in Luke 15:19 are the most powerful words that Prodigal can speak to Betrayed to ensure he or she has experienced a radical change of heart. Those words eliminate any attempt to rationalize or confabulate some excuse for betrayal. "I have sinned" sets the mood for real, honest admission of guilt by Prodigal. It is a verbal parallel to waving a white flag of surrender. "I have sinned" says I have no hidden agenda, no ulterior motive, and no reasonable excuse for my adultery and no false expectation of being exonerated for my transgression.

When Prodigal manifests this transparency and admits the betrayal was sinful behavior, it acts as a catalyst for the dynamics of real reconciliation to begin. Now, Betrayed has to begin working through the denial, deception, grief, and anger as these emotions all hit him or her at once. As Job is quoted in his book, "The thing I greatly feared has come upon me," so every spouse deals with at least a subliminal apprehension that someday he or she will be confronted by their greatest fear: *betrayal.*

After many years of counseling and dealing with innumerable cases of infidelity, there is one situation that is forever forged in my memory. It occurred the day a minister confided that he recently confronted his wife with his suspicions, and she had confessed to her adultery. In the next breath, she stated that she could be pregnant with her lover's baby. In his moments of overwhelming grief and despair, he had to accompany her for a pregnancy test while praying fervently it would be negative. If ever insult was added to injury, this was the time, and his pain seemed unbearable.

I have never witnessed a person more broken or crushed in spirit than this minister. Perhaps it was because he is a fellow minister that I felt such compassion for him. He was still dealing with the brutal news of his wife's recent betrayal, the possibility of an illegitimate child, whether his marriage could survive, whether he wanted it to survive, whether their children should be told, if his home could remain intact, if his wife's adultery would become public knowledge, if his church should be informed, and if his ministry would survive this devastation. All of the aftermath of his wife's adultery bombarded him simultaneously. It caused him to spiral rapidly downward into a dark chasm of anguish he had never before known. It was only by the daily grace of God this man was surviving.

Unless you have had experience in counseling couples dealing with infidelity, or you have experienced this devastation firsthand, you might never be able to understand or empathize with the depths of this man's sorrow and torment. He described how the very thoughts of his beloved wife in the arms and the bed of another man made him writhe and wail in uncontrollable grief. The images that haunted him night and day were debilitating. He wept profusely.

This minister admitted he was unable to think, socialize,

eat, pray, or preach. Demonic spirits taunted and tantalized him constantly, and he, like some in the Bible, daily prayed to die. Depression with its accompanying offsprings of Withdrawal, Apathy, and Loss of Productivity drove this energetic, athletic, and congenial man to the brink of suicide.

He felt that the crushing blow of infidelity had rendered him to be nothing more than "a dead man walking." Amid the uncontrollable tears and gut-wrenching sobs, he uttered the words I shall never forget, "My heart died the day I discovered her adultery. I'm just waiting for my body to catch up!"

God, in His infinite grace and mercy, answered his prayers about the pregnancy test, and no baby came from her illicit union. Thankfully, through her admission of guilt, sincere repentance, and her resultant spiritual restoration, they renewed their vows. It was a significant step toward believing their home and marriage could be saved.

This ministry couple then committed themselves to confidential Christian counseling, and their marriage was eventually restored. After a much-needed sabbatical, including a great deal of prayer and ministry to his wife, he has been able to resume his fulltime ministry. His wife now lives an unimpeachable, Christlike life and stands devotedly beside him in his calling. They have not forgotten her sin, but she is forgiven. Because of our professional and personal closeness, their case became the defining motivation for this story of the *Prodigal Spouse*.

The intensity and sincerity of a prodigal's confession and repentance will be the most critical element in determining the amount of time needed for the recovery of the marriage. Prodigals must admit his or her sin against God, his or her spouse, and family. He or she must acknowledge his or her moral and spiritual failures without hesitation or qualification. Then, he or she can ask for mercy and forgiveness from

God and Betrayed. The pain will not immediately disappear, but it will be tempered by the sincerity and intensity of the contrition Prodigal demonstrates.

13

recompense

"I am no more worthy to be called your son, make me as one of your servants."

Luke 15:19

Restitution and recompense are now the sole responsibility of Prodigal. His or her moral failure has brought an end to the marriage: if not legally, then certainly functionally. In addition, he or she may have brought shame, reproach, insecurity, infidelity, shattered trust, grief, and the sexual history of a third party into the marriage. Prodigal must prepare to make amends for his or her actions of betrayal. It will not be easy, and it certainly will not be swift.

There is no quick fix for a broken marriage. Prodigal needs to understand that the relationship he or she shattered with betrayal may take years to restore. Actually, it *will* take years to restore fully. Prodigal must face up to his or her sin and begin the process on the long road to restoration of the marriage. The prodigal has caused unbelievable pain and anguish with his or her betrayal, and he or she must accept the responsibility for his or her actions.

I cannot repeat this enough because most prodigals want this process of reconciliation to be an *event* that is quickly concluded. Restoration is just not going to happen that way. Prodigal, you are going to get weary of having to live every moment of every day with the responsibility of restoration sitting squarely upon your shoulders. This stage of the process is where many prodigals simply quit. Rebuilding a fractured relationship is more difficult than forming a new one, and Prodigal can grow tired and frustrated by the perceived demands placed upon him or her for reconstruction of the marriage.

Since fidelity and trust are the foundations of a marriage, restoration cannot be limited to only the aesthetics or the surface issues. It must plumb the depths of the relationship until it reaches the very bedrock upon which marriage is based. This takes time and effort on the part of the couple.

The one motivation that will keep Prodigal from quitting is the intensity of commitment he or she has to the healing of Betrayed's broken heart. This part of the reconciliation is about Betrayed. Prodigal must humble himself or herself and face the repercussions of his or her adultery. Since Prodigal broke the vows, he or she must restore the sanctity of the marriage covenant. Otherwise, Betrayed will never again trust Prodigal, and a marriage without trust is doomed.

Prodigal, at this time you may be considered *unworthy* of your former position in the marriage, but you are certainly not *worthless*. Your sin has disqualified you from the former level of unquestioned trust you enjoyed in the marriage. Your position with Betrayed has been severely compromised by your adultery, and there are lasting consequences from your sin. The good news is that with God's help, your trustworthiness can eventually be restored.

For your spouse to be able to trust you again will require

your commitment to the hard work of submission. Prodigal, you must be willing to be accountable for your actions and whereabouts twenty-four hours a day, seven days a week. There can be *no* exceptions if you want restoration.

Just remember, Prodigal, you no longer get a free pass on questionable behavior or inaccessibility. A tarnished character extracts a heavy toll, and you will have to pay. This does not occur because Betrayed is vindictive, but because you have destroyed your trustworthiness. Your every action or absence is now under the microscope. For a while, you will not receive the "benefit of the doubt." Those days of being unaccountable for your whereabouts or your conduct are history. Face it, Prodigal, you simply cannot be trusted now! God commands us to love one another, but we are not commanded to trust. Trust is an earned benefit in any relationship.

How can Prodigal begin the process of recompensing Betrayed and having his or her trust restored? What are some practical things Prodigal can do to help diminish the pain he or she has caused and find a panacea for his or her marriage? The answer to these poignant questions is surprisingly simple. I have entitled this process "The Prodigal's Pledge." It contains ten powerful insights.

The Prodigal's Pledge provides a workable plan that will demonstrate his or her commitment to restoring Betrayed's trust if he or she will promise to comply.

1. First and foremost, pledge to display your unconditional love for your spouse. Realize how blessed you are to be in love with someone who obviously loves and cares about you. Say "I love you" often and in different ways. Surprise Betrayed with gifts or tokens of your love to express your feelings for him or her. Keep in mind that love grows in an atmo-

sphere of freedom and trust, not from duty or obligation. Do not ever take your spouse's love for granted. Love is a gift we give, not a shackle we wear. Help Betrayed fall in love with you all over again.

2. Pledge yourself to listen with the same attention as you would a dear friend. Acceptance is a key to understanding and a buffer for tension and resentment. Do not take things personally when your spouse has a different opinion or perception. Allow yourselves the right to disagree. If you do not want someone to control your feelings, do not try to control theirs. Allow some emotional latitude for Betrayed to deal with his or her pain while observing your consistent actions of love.

3. Pledge never to stop treating your spouse like your sweetheart. Talk to him or her as your sweetheart, not your adversary. Do things that sweethearts do. Offer to assist him or her in his or her work or chores. Keep working together toward common goals. Do things just to make your spouse feel loved, especially if he or she is having a bad day or feeling sad. Take pride in the way you look and act without appearing salacious or promiscuous.

4. Pledge to take care of your spouse. Be available to accompany your spouse to the doctor, run errands, pick up prescriptions, prepare a special meal for him or her when he or she needs some extra tender loving care. Put the other person first, but do not neglect your own needs. Do things that show you are interested

in your spouse and that not only did your body come home, but your heart is there also.

5. Make a pledge to look to your spouse as your first line of help or defense against problems or temptations. Do not allow anything or anyone to cause you to seek someone else as a confidant or a companion. This is time for extreme exclusivity between you and your spouse. Be thankful that you have someone you can talk with. Be grateful that there is a mutual commitment to work through times of sickness, poverty, pain, or whatever other problems may arise.

Realize the two of you are in this life together, so maximize your marriage benefits. Ecclesiastes 4:9–10 says, "Two *are* better than one; because they have a good reward for their labour. For if they fall, the one will lift up his fellow: but woe to him *that is* alone when he falleth; for *he hath* not another to help him up." Thank God for *Couple Power*! Utilize this God-given dynamic by partnering in prayer and care for one another.

6. Pledge to talk about things the way you would with your dearest, closest friend. Refuse to criticize or speak negatively to or about your spouse, no matter how he or she may be acting. His or her pain is real, and it will not dissipate quickly, so you must be considerate and consistent in your pledge of allegiance to them. Share your most important secrets and never betray your spouse's. Trust will never be restored if

you are found guilty of violating your spouse's confidentiality after you have violated your marriage vows. Through it all, do not give up on your love, your spouse, your marriage, or your quest for complete restoration.

7. Pledge yourself to settle the fact and declare it often to Betrayed that you have made your choice and you want to spend the rest of your life with him or her. You do not want nor need anyone else, and your prodigal days are over *forever*. Do whatever it takes to convince them of this promise you are making. Never allow yourself to be flirtatious, because you now know the horrible consequences that can occur. Keep fidelity as the most important goal of your marriage.

8. Pledge to be agreeable about decisions that involve the marriage. There will be plenty of time to fine-tune the details for decision making in your relationship. At this point, your infidelity displayed a major lack of wisdom and intelligence on your part. Therefore, Betrayed has valid reasons to question your decision-making ability. Give Betrayed time and be willing to submit your decisions for his or her input. You are neither a child nor a doormat, but your credibility will remain under scrutiny until you prove yourself trustworthy again. Do not grow impatient in the process.

9. When you are in doubt about Betrayed's reactions, simply ask how you would want to be treated if the roles were reversed. If you argue, do not go to sleep without resolving the issue.

Ask for forgiveness when you make a mistake, even if you do not want to or feel like it. It shows you are sincere about your feelings for Betrayed and how he or she is coping with the circumstances.

Pledge to do whatever will bring mutual happiness for the remainder of the marriage: first Betrayed's happiness and then yours. In every case, do what is best for your spouse and your goal of re-establishing his or her trust in you.

10. Lastly, pledge to be fun to be with and make the environment a fun place for both of you. Both of you know that behind that smile is the stigmata of the *Scarlet Letter* as an ever-present reminder of your sin. This should fade in time if you will maintain your unwavering commitment to Betrayed and the sanctity of your marriage. No matter what occurs, keep your "Prodigal's Pledge" and you will be rewarded with the love, loyalty, and the trust of your spouse.

reconciliation

"The father had compassion and ran...and kissed him continuously."

Luke 15:20

The return and repentance of Prodigal present a mixed bag of emotions for Betrayed. On the one hand, he or she may feel the relief of rediscovering Prodigal. The lost spouse has been found since Prodigal has safely returned. During Prodigal's absence, Betrayed has had time to dream about what the reunion would be like. Now, Betrayed is faced with the reality of dealing with the aftermath of adultery.

Responsibility for the future of the marriage now shifts squarely to the shoulders of the victim. Since Prodigal has returned and been repentant, the parameters for reconciliation are transferred to Betrayed. Betrayed is the victim of adultery. He or she is the one who suffered the infidelity of his or her spouse with the attendant fears, anger, distress, and hopelessness that accompany such betrayals.

Betrayed was sinned against by the adultery of Prodigal. Since Prodigal has come home, only the victim can decide if or when reconciliation will occur. Betrayed has the right to terminate the marriage if he or she desires. The Bible gives him or her this option. Betrayed now hold all the cards.

Betrayed's reaction to the disclosure of the infidelity will set one of two dynamics into motion. Either the repairing of or the dissolution of the marriage will become his or her stated goal. If the objective is repairing the marriage, it probably has very little to do with Betrayed's true feelings. Feelings at this stage can fool you. Betrayed may feel overwhelmed with relief or consumed with rage. Neither emotion should be the motivator for what course of action is taken. These initial emotions are not accurate barometers as a catalyst for Betrayed's reaction.

The intensity of Betrayed's responses will be affected by the sincerity and conviction of the repentant Prodigal. If there were ever a time in the process of reconciliation to be transparent, it is now. Failure to disclose past problems or unhappiness probably contributed to the pursuant infidelity by Prodigal. Truth may hurt in the moment, but it is by far the best course of action in reconciling the marriage. If Betrayed is *truly* happy that Prodigal has returned, he or she should expose his or her vulnerability and show it.

Prodigal is anxiously awaiting Betrayed's response. A moment can seem like a lifetime when awaiting a reaction. Just as Prodigal had time to ponder the homecoming, so Betrayed has had time to imagine what this moment would be like. He or she has had opportunity to role-play the reunion and predetermine how he or she would respond to a returning, repentant Prodigal. Now is the time for Betrayed to act from his or her heart, not just his or her head.

Your mind might be inclined to use self-defense mechanisms to protect yourself from being blindsided again. Betrayed may want to demand assurances from Prodigal *before* accepting his or her act of contrition. However, true love will not seek retribution and reprisal, no matter how intensely it desires to. Nor will true love make the repentant heart squirm and beg for forgiveness. True love seeks to reconcile and rebuild despite the pain it is presently experiencing.

Never will the magnitude of Betrayed's character be more vividly on display than when confronted with the options of determining Prodigal's future. Betrayed now possesses an unbridled power over Prodigal that was not evident before. It has been said, "Absolute power absolutely corrupts." The essence of the quotation means that few people can handle being *sovereign*. The privilege of making unilateral, uncontested decisions without being accountable to anyone can destroy even the most well-meaning person. Betrayed now gets to make the decision as to whether he or she wants reconciliation with Prodigal.

In a moment, Betrayed's life has run the gamut, from feeling totally powerless to feeling totally powerful. This is something he or she never thought would happen. The power of choice was with Prodigal. He or she called the shots, made the choices, and forced Betrayed to live with the results. Now the authority to decide destinies belongs to Betrayed. The role of judge, jury, and executioner are all in his or her hands. Betrayed was handed the gavel when Prodigal admitted and repented of the sin of adultery. What happens next is critical to the future of this marriage.

Our biblical paradigm in Luke 15 shows us the ultimate gift of acceptance for an erring and prodigal mate. Betrayed casts aside all claims for immediate explanations and assurances as he or she witnesses the sincere guilt, brokenness, and shame of Prodigal. The focus is not, "Where have you been?" but, "Thank God you're home." Christ's story tells us that the father had compassion on his prodigal son. He allowed his feelings *for* his son's return to override his feeling *against* his son's prodigality.

There is a discipline of selfless love demanded by our Lord, which must be tapped into at this stage. It finds its source in something far deeper than mere human emotions. Betrayed must exhibit strong, positive, compassionate feelings for the beloved Prodigal. This expression of love and care does not deny the existence of serious questions and concerns about the adulterous behavior. While Betrayed can *admit* to having these negative feelings, he or she must not *submit* to them during the initial reconciliation process.

The next behavior exhibited by the father in the text is the conjoining of "approaching" and "affection." The Bible says he ran and kissed him continuously. No one would question Betrayed's right to confront and condemn Prodigal for what he or she has put him or her through, but that is not the appropriate behavior for reconciliation. Prodigal's actions were reprehensible; he or she has admitted it. Prodigal has now done everything he or she can do. Now Prodigal must wait for Betrayed to respond.

It is at this point the principles of Logic and Scripture merge. The two primary words that describe Betrayed's options are *protasis* and *apodosis*. These words stem from the syllogism of a conditional clause. The first simply means "If you will ..." followed by *apodosis*, which means "Then I will ..." They represent a conditional promise that is based upon the action of the first person followed by the response of the second person.

This conditional clause is clearly seen in the passage from 2 Chronicles 7:14, where it reads, "*If* my people, which are called by my name, shall humble themselves, and pray, and seek my face, and turn from their wicked ways; *then* will I hear from heaven, and will forgive their sin, and will heal their land" (emphases mine). God Himself used the "If/ Then" syllogism of conditional response as He told Israel, "If you will pray, then I will hear and heal." Since Prodigal demonstrated the protasis by repenting, it is now incumbent upon Betrayed to perform the apodosis and forgive.

What I saw when I put this conditional syllogism under the microscope was a matter of focus. In the Suzerainty-vassal covenant, of which the Bible provides the prototype within the strict confines of the Berith (Old Testament Covenant), both the protasis and apodosis are required for the success of the arrangement.

In the Bible, the king represented the Suzerain or a bene-factor who must provide, without delay or withdrawal, all the benefits upon which h*e initiated* the Covenant. The vassals were the subjects or the beneficiaries of the covenant bless-ings. They agreed to maintain their loyalty and devotion to the king.

The king could not be capricious and vacillate in his role without coming under the sentence of death upon which this type of Covenant was hinged. The same was true of the vassal's consequences should they choose to break the Covenant with their king. Both parties had to swear "Unto Death" to maintain the Covenant at all costs. God's covenant with Abraham, recorded in Genesis 15 (Hebrew text), shows the aspects of this covenant ceremony.

The Suzerainty-vassal Covenant was a two-party agree-ment, and both parties had rights and responsibilities in order for the Covenant not to be voided. Since God states that He will never void or vacate His portion of the agree-ment (Psalms 89:34), the focus shifts to the vassals to make sure that they do not void or vacate the Berith (Jewish Covenant). If it cannot be voided by one or both of the par-ties by a decision of their choosing, then it is not a Berith. It would be a dictum by an emperor where the vassals become *slaves*, not subjects of the king.

God initiated the first covenant with man. His next order of business was to establish a Marriage Covenant between a man and a woman that reflected the same Suzerainty-vassal or protasis-apodosis qualities as His covenant. The husband was deemed to be the leader and thereby the initiator of the covenant. The wife would then be afforded all of the benefits of his love, devotion, and protection.

The feature of "If you will, then I will" condition is paramount to understanding the relationships in a covenant of marriage. In Prodigal's return, he or she has fulfilled the first portion of the conditional syllogism demanded of the vassal: he or she has repented. Since Prodigal has repented and satisfied his or her responsibility, the ball is now in Betrayed's court as the Suzerain to fulfill the apodosis and forgive his or her trespass.

If Betrayed will mirror the behavior of the father, the reconciliation process will take a quantum leap forward. Prodigal will be anxious to see the level of caution or resistance Betrayed shows. Prodigal may not run to Betrayed's arms for fear of rejection and further humiliation as possible fallout from his or her sin. It is a consummate joy for Prodigal to see the one he or she betrayed running *toward* and not away from him or her. The act of continuously kissing and hugging Prodigal is the ultimate "welcome home" sign. Betrayed is ignoring the pain and offering pardon.

This stage is not the time for a platonic peck on the cheek. This is the time for Betrayed to convey love, affection, forgiveness, and reconciliation to the wayward and weary Prodigal, even though he or she may not feel like it. Betrayed's reception of the returning Prodigal is based upon faith and forgiveness, not feelings.

The trip home for Prodigal was filled with excruciating fears and self-loathing, but with every hug and every kiss comes a welcomed relief. Prodigal knows that Betrayed has every right to consider himself or herself as a victim, injured, betrayed, or offended, but right now all that matters is knowing that Betrayed still cares. Betrayed has been wounded deeply but musters the grace to say, "I choose to forgive you."

restoration

"Robe, ring, and shoes." Luke 15:22

"For better or worse" is sometimes worse. Well, actually, it is *usually* worse. The primary factor causing this condition is that most couples do not continue the masquerade of pre-marital courtship. The bride is shocked to discover that the groom no longer speaks in sentences. He usually grunts or groans. In her estimation, any conversation involving polysyllabic words is a major breakthrough in dialogue. His charm meter just got *worse*.

The groom is in for a rude awakening when he discovers that his bride is not wired the same as he is sexually. All of his prenuptial fantasies about frequent, uninhibited, mutually mind-blowing, bed-rattling sex met the reality of being married to someone who didn't find laundry, cleaning, and cooking very arousing. Her erotic meter just got *worse*.

Worse does not end there. Worse can include many of the characteristics described earlier under the heading of "Obnoxious Behavior." Worse for one couple was when the wife said to her husband, "I didn't think you could get angry."

Which is worse in that case, the husband's concealed temper or the wife's naiveté?

Who would go into a marriage thinking his or her spouse could never get angry? The same type of person who thinks the temperature of his or her love life is going to remain on "boil" after the honeymoon. This is just a sampling of data that proves marriage can be full of surprises. Some are for better, many are for worse.

Worse, thankfully, does not mean "the end." Worse is just a marital synonym for "normal." Every honest couple will tell you that *some* things did get worse after they were married. Otherwise, why would that phrase be included in the ceremony? That is a tip-off right there to the prudent couple as to what may happen in the marriage. It does not have to be the fault of either spouse for something to get worse. It is simply a natural consequence of two people living together within the union of marriage.

The Bible is replete with examples of marital difficulties or discord. Couples like Adam and Eve (eating off each other's plates), Abraham and Sarah (messing with your wife's *things*), Isaac and Rebecca (keeping secrets and playing favorites), Moses and Zipporah (having to do your husband's chores), David and Michal (embarrassing your spouse in public), Solomon and his seven hundred plural marriage partners ("Why didn't you tell me your beliefs *before* we were married?"), Hosea and Gomer ("You're acting just like your mother!"), Joseph and Mary ("You can't touch me this year."), and many others were familiar with the challenges of being married to an opposite. God did not hide these vignettes of marital struggles from us in His Word.

When the minister states in the ceremony, "You two shall become one," he did not tell the couple that the hardest part of their marriage would be deciding which *one* they would become. Each individual will subconsciously attempt to make the spouse more like themselves. The wife wants her husband to think and feel as she does. Of course, the husband desires the same behavioral modification from his wife. Marriage ceremonies are usually conducted at an altar, not an *alter*. Becoming "one" means that both persons must allow themselves to be altered with the new "oneness," being a new entity created by God.

The originator of the marriage ceremony understood that, while marriage can be idyllic, it is not *utopia* (Greek, "nowhere, no place"). There is "no place" where everything is perfect except heaven. Do not even begin to think that your marriage is going to be perfect. The reason is clear: it involves two imperfect people. Two imperfects do not create anything perfect. By all means, you should shoot for the stars, but understand if you come up a bit short. Lowell once said, "It isn't failure that is the problem, it is low aim." So, aim high for the perfect marriage but realize that most never attain it.

Now we know why the minister makes us repeat our vows to one another. Because if you didn't, you might go AWOL at the first hint of trouble your marriage experiences. These are vows to love, honor, and cherish. They certainly may be tested, but your vows should never be discarded. Our vows were made in the presence of God and witnesses. You need that kind of accountability when it comes to your commitment to marriage. You need the reminder of your friends, family, and God when things get worse and you feel like bailing on the marriage.

The prodigal did bail. He or she chose to ignore the vows he or she had made before God, leaving a trail of broken hearts, broken lives, and a broken home. In the midst of this horrendous period of time, the victim of the betrayal is given the sacred privilege of restoring the erring prodigal mate to his or her previous marital position. This is grace and mercy in action. This is the time to act like the father in Luke 15. This is the time to act like God when the erring ones come hobbling home.

The adulterer was willing to come back and be as a hired servant with no position, no rights, and no respect. Prodigal knows he or she has broken the covenant made on his or her wedding day and has jeopardized the marriage. Prodigal knows he or she has neither rights nor demands that he or she can enforce *if* he or she is repentant and recompensing.

Repentance does not allow for a plea bargain. Prodigals cannot say he or she will repent *if* certain criteria are met or certain penalties are taken off the table. Honest repentance is based on sorrow for sin, not diminished consequences promised by the victim.

Prodigal has already realized that the worst place in the world is to be in the "far country" feeding swine. *That* was the low life! What could Betrayed demand of the repentant prodigal that would seem too high of a cost to pay for his or her adultery? When Prodigal keeps focused on what he or she has done to Betrayed, he or she will be willing to accept any terms or caveats Betrayed demands for the process of restoration to proceed.

Nevertheless, Betrayed says, "I do not accept your offer. No spouse of mine will be a hired servant in *our* house." In one statement, Betrayed shows the magnanimous attitude of a forgiver. Betrayed's view is not to punish but to restore. He or she seals the moment by saying, "You were my mate *before*, and you will be my mate *again*. Here are the emblems of your restored position. I have this *robe* to cover you from the exposure of your sin. I have this *ring* for you to show that you have been restored to a place of authority, not subservience, in our home. I have these *shoes* for you to show that you will never be mistaken for my servant but my spouse."

Somewhere in the heart of Betrayed was a belief that Prodigal would return. As an action of that faith, Betrayed apparently had the emblems ready for Prodigal's return. There was no hurried trip to Wal-Mart for a robe. There was no stopping by "Pic and Pay" for some new shoes. There was no urgent call to "The Jewelry Box" to inquire if they had a signet ring in stock. Betrayed was ready for his or her part in the scenario of restoration. This is a great lesson in faith: Prepare for what you are praying for, and don't be surprised when it arrives!

Prodigal can now thank God that there is no "Scarlet Letter" in Father's house. It is well deserved, but mercy has erased it. Instead of a condemning monogram proclaiming his or her guilt, there is a robe proclaiming his or her pardon. Prodigal has come home where he or she belongs. There will be no public humiliation for the infidelity, just a robe, a ring, and new shoes telling everyone that the beloved prodigal has come home, and home was waiting for the prodigal.

Compassion tempers condemnation on the part of the innocent spouse. Unbearable pain is met with supernatural pardon, and God's grace is proving sufficient for each day of the process … one day at a time.

16

rejoicing

" … my son was dead, and is alive again; he was lost, and
is found. And they began to be merry."

Luke 15:24

There is no rejoicing over sin, but there is ecstasy over salvation. There is no rejoicing over rebellion, but there is elation
over reunion. There is no rejoicing over infidelity, but there
is joyful anticipation over the prospects of renewed intimacy.
After the initial hugs and kisses welcoming the prodigal
home comes the celebration of restoration.

Celebration seemed like such a distant memory for
Betrayed. Perhaps the wedding reception provided a time of
festivities for him or her, but those memories seemed blurred
by the events of infidelity. It is difficult to imagine a celebration when tears of sorrow stain his or her pillow each night.
These tears are a result of the incessant bombardment of the
lurid and detestable images of his or her spouse in his or her
lover's bed. These thoughts of Prodigal and a party seem
incongruent. Betrayed's constant companion had been pain,
not jubilation.

But that was then and this is now! Pain is eased by the anticipation of pleasure as the erring one has come home. What had seemed lost forever is now found. The love that felt dead is rekindled. The joy of reunion is overwhelming. It is everything Betrayed *prayed* for; it is everything Prodigal *hoped* for. Neither one knew for certain it would ever happen, but it has. The depths of despair Betrayed felt when Prodigal left are contrasted by the heights of exhilaration he or she feels seeing Prodigal again. A repentant Prodigal is being welcomed home by an embracing spouse.

Where Prodigal had hungered for husks, he or she now smells the pit-cooked aroma of the fatted calf. The *best* one in the herd was saved in anticipation of this moment. This is his or her very own banquet given by the very person he or she betrayed with his or her infidelity. This is an enormous expression of love, forgiveness, and acceptance. Forgiveness has been called "life's eraser," and Betrayed is offering this amazing, self-sacrificing gift to Prodigal. None of this is deserved, but it is appreciated and certainly enjoyed.

Many spouses faced with infidelity want to wait until they *feel* like forgiving the erring spouse before he or she embraces the returning prodigal. Forgiveness is not a "feeling-first" dynamic. Forgiveness has actually been described as a *promise we give*, not a *feeling* we have. If you wait until you feel like forgiving the person who betrayed you, you may never forgive him or her of his or her trespasses against you.

Many would ask, "Exactly what is this promise we make when we grant forgiveness?" Dr. Jay Adams, in his book *Competent to Counsel*, gives perhaps the clearest working answer to this question. Dr. Adams says forgiveness is a threefold promise to the transgressor. (1) I promise never to bring up your sin to you again, (2) I promise not to bring it up to others, and (3) I promise I will not dwell on it myself.

This threefold promise has absolutely nothing to do with your feelings. Be assured, your forgiveness of Prodigal will not be based upon an absence of negative emotions you are processing. Your forgiveness must be based on higher principles than human emotions. Jealousy, anger, rage, grief, frustration, aggravation, and bitterness are more likely to be your concomitant feelings when you see Prodigal return. However, those emotions will not produce the fruit of forgiveness in your heart.

What happens when you make this threefold promise of forgiveness to someone? You set in motion the exploration of a *trail* that will eventually lead you to a place of healing for your broken heart. Be advised, at times it will be extremely difficult to keep the promise. In fact, it will seem practically impossible to keep the promise in the early stages of reconciliation. Betrayeds often fail to keep one or more of these promises on a day-to-day basis. Just do not give up! This is your road to recovery, and the journey is an ongoing one.

When you err and make a reference to Prodigal about his or her sin, you will probably experience the compunction of your conscience. This is God's gentle reminder that He knows what will help you expedite your healing. He knew long before psychologists that "what you verbalize is what you reinforce." In other words, what you *think* about is what you *talk* about, and what you *talk* about is what you *think* about. Unless controlled, this cycle of painful thoughts and words will hinder you from ever receiving your healing from the anguish of adultery.

The reciprocal of this principle is also true. When you discipline yourself to think about forgiveness, reconciliation, and reunion, your words will flow from that fountain of healing thoughts. The most marvelous aspect of the biblical principle is that your thoughts and words are not dependant upon your feelings. In fact, when you function in this discipline, *you* will determine your feelings. Your thoughts produce your words, and they, in turn, produce your feelings. Your thoughts are the words you speak to yourself. Therefore, to *feel* good you must *think* good thoughts and *speak* good, wholesome words (see Philippians 4:8).

Just as when most of us betrayed our Heavenly Father and left home, the things Prodigal went searching for in the far country were *in* Father's house all the time. Prodigal just could not see what was there because of the lure of temptation. Now the futile search is over; the long road of ruin is behind. Betrayed has shown forgiveness and is restoring Prodigal. Now it is time to rejoice. The prodigal has migrated from dishonor back to honor, from swine to shoes, from riotous living to a robe, from debauchery to dancing, from disgrace to God's grace.

All of this merriment became possible because Prodigal came to himself or herself and returned home. As the prodigal looks around in amazement, he or she realizes that all of this fellowship, food, and merriment is for him or her. He or she must never, ever allow himself or herself to hunger for the husks of the far country again.

Many couples have understandably faced the thoughts of restoration and the reintegration of Prodigal into the marriage with fear and uncertainty. It is one thing to learn principles and paradigms, but couples yearn for some practical application they can really grasp.

One of the simplest, yet most profound answers I have shared is the image of a bicycle wheel. This visual is easy for everyone to embrace. The diagram I draw features the normal elements: the wheel, the spokes, and the hub, but with a little ball on two of the spokes to represent each spouse.

In the worst-case scenario, I draw the two balls at the

extreme edge of the wheel, as far from the hub as they can get, and totally opposite each other. This describes the way many marriages seem after a severe crisis. The couple has two options facing them. They can try to get as close together as they can on their own by negotiating the differences. This plan does not have a great success ratio because the focus is on the distance apart, and how to negotiate a merger of polar opposites. As has been mentioned earlier, many people want to enjoy the success but will not commit to the *process* for attaining it

The merger can be successfully negotiated by simply changing the perspective from "how do we bridge the great gulf that separates us?" to "what is there in the middle that is attractive to both of us?" When a couple decides they will make God the Hub of their life and marriage and move toward Him, no matter how far apart they are, as they get closer to the Hub, they will get closer to each other. The goal is to meet in the middle and have God as the center of the individuals as well as the hub around which the marriage revolves. It is simple physics: Get closer to God (the Hub) and you get closer to each other.

Somewhere in the catacombs of their minds, both spouses may wonder about their future and if this "Spoke Theory" really works. You will never know unless you give it a try.

"Surely our marriage cannot be a party forever, now can it?" they ponder. Neither mate wants the illicit passions and pursuits of the prodigal ever to resurface again. But that thought is for another day. Prodigal has returned. Today is Homecoming! Home, sweet home.

17

remembering

"But as soon as this thy son was come, which hath devoured thy living with harlots…"

Luke 15:30

Memories will be one of the greatest challenges the couple will face in the aftermath of adultery. As hard as they try, there will be sights, sounds, smells, locations, names, and other stimuli that will trigger a rush of painful memories. For the repentant Prodigal, his or her emotions will typically center on guilt. For the forgiving Betrayed, his or her emotions will be the replay of desertion, sorrow, and pain, and the haunting fear of a recurring betrayal.

The ultimate goal of this book, should you decide to accept it, is to help each of you to reach the place regarding the betrayal where you can *revisit the events without rewinding the effects*. Please be advised, you will both have times when your thoughts will take you back in time to the crisis of infidelity you have come through.

You can have periodic occasions when you remember the events of the betrayal, but you, thankfully, are not "re-feeling" the emotions of the betrayal. You can go *to* it without going *through* it again. The wounds can heal, but the scars will remain. Just remember, the good news is that scars do not hurt!

Many couples have indicated that the rest of their lives, they dealt with painful memories. The good news is that the more repentant and the more forgiving the couple is toward each other, the more the memories tend to dissipate with time. Contrary to common folklore, time *does not* heal. Medically speaking, time actually contributes to infection. Therefore, you must be proactive in the battle with unpleasant memories if you want to control their effect upon you. You must learn to change your focus when painful memories come rushing in.

Professional photographers deal with different types of lenses in order to shape the framing and composition of the image on the film or digital file. A micro or close-up lens will remove all the surrounding elements so that you only see a very minute area in the photograph. This allows the photographer to single out and display one petal from the rest of the flower or one leaf from a tree. This lens magnifies the details in the subject that otherwise would go unnoticed. The frame is filled with this tiny detail, previously overlooked, but now greatly magnified in the portrait.

Conversely, the wide-angle lens shows the whole setting of the garden or orchard without specific attention given to the fine details of a single element. The photographer wants you to see the whole scene in its context, not fixate upon one drop of water on a leaf or a speck of nectar dripping from the flower. This photograph keeps everything in its proper perspective as it relates to its surroundings.

Managing your memories will require you to attempt to keep the "big picture" in focus during the restoration process.

Putting Prodigal's every detail of adultery under the microscope will only enhance and enlarge the degree of difficulty Betrayed will experience in recovery. Prodigal must also guard against fixating upon a weakness or misstep by Betrayed and keep his or her eyes on the larger framework of recovery. Both must work at keeping things in the context of reconciliation. Both will be tempted to scrutinize every element of minutiae from the infidelity. Betrayed, for your own wellbeing and that of Prodigal, steer clear of your micro lens.

It will become evident upon initiating the process of recovery that there will always be someone in the vicinity who believes it is his or her duty to remind you of the infidelity. He or she will say that he or she is well meaning, but you will soon discover that his or her true motive is to rub the situation in your face. He or she does not plan to ever forget the adultery, and he or she certainly does not want Prodigal or Betrayed to forget it either.

Betrayed, there are people who will go out of their way to tell you how wrong you are for accepting Prodigal back into your marriage. These highly skilled skeptics may even go so far as to cite *The Septuagint's* quotation of Solomon in Proverbs 19:22 saying, "He that keeps an adulteress is foolish and ungodly." Betrayed, you must weigh that statement against the account of the Prophet Hosea. He was instructed by God to buy his unfaithful wife out of slavery and bring her home. She was a *repeat-offender* adulteress whose mother was a prostitute, and yet God saw something about the situation that man did not see. While both of these Scriptures portray the offender as a woman, the principle would equally apply should the offender be a man.

Prodigal, if your sin has been uncovered, you will be the subject of unmerciful gossip. Friends, family, neighbors, and coworkers will all have their part in dissecting your behavior.

Depending on your location, you may very well become the talk of the town or the church. Adultery is not like getting a parking ticket or returning a book to the library past the due date. In most of society and nearly all of Christianity, adultery is considered a capital offense, and *you* are the felon. Someone will try to make you do "hard time" *for* your sin. What they do not realize is that you already did "hard time" *during* your sin.

In our biblical account by Christ in Luke 15, He shared one more element of the story for our consideration. This last view is that of the elder brother, the one who stayed home, the one who worked hard, the one who never strayed or squandered his earnings, the one who despised "wasteful-ness." These are the characteristics of the elder brother we are discussing.

When Prodigal came home, not everyone was happy. The "I told you so's" did not want to see Prodigal come home. For whatever his or her reasons, he or she liked it better with him or her out of the picture. We do not know what was in the brother's heart, but what came out of his mouth was pure venom. Upon hearing and seeing the celebration and smell-ing the barbeque on the fire, this elder brother issued his disclaimer regarding the whole celebration scene.

He distanced himself from his younger brother, Prodigal, when talking to his father by referring to him as "thy son." He reminds his father of what a noble and faithful son he has always been. Then, he makes sure his father's memory does not fail him regarding Prodigal's escapade. The Elder brother is a prime example of those who are determined to keep you from forgetting the horrible sin of your spouse and your perceived stupidity for restoring him or her.

In our biblical reference, it was the action of the older brother that showed disdain for his prodigal brother. It is obvious from his statement that he was also showing some degree of contempt for his father. The older brother felt he could see right through the sham and wanted his father to put Prodigal in his rightful place by rejecting his repentance.

If you noticed carefully, he makes a very accurate statement; however, it is done in a very condemning context. He tells his father that Prodigal has "devoured *thy* living with harlots" (emphasis mine). All of this is true. Prodigal was wasteful. Prodigal did take something that had been shared *with* him and shared it in illicit, sexual liaisons. All true, every word of it. The older brother hit the nail on the head, but his motives were obviously wrong. He wanted to shame the prodigal for his sin and manipulate his father into rejecting his repentant brother.

Betrayed, one of the hurdles in managing your memories is that you are going to have to deal with the fact that your spouse took something very special that you shared together and gave it to another. Then, upon reuniting with you, he or she brought something he or she shared with a "harlot," and now part of "New Lover" is in your home.

You can never undo the destruction to the monogamous relationship you and Prodigal previously enjoyed. Your future will forever be linked to the harlots of Prodigal's past. This is a painful and inescapable truth. However, that truth focused on under the micro lens will destroy any possibility of restoration. You must avoid the temptation to obsess upon this if you intend to ever recover from the haunting memories of infidelity.

Prodigal, you and Betrayed do not need the help of others to remember your situation. If no one ever breathed a word to you, you still must deal with your conscience, your painful memories, and your feelings of guilt. Then, there is Satan, who will always be close by to condemn you for your failures. Your memories will be one of your greatest challenges. They will be your greatest personal battleground for recovery. The simple way to fast-track this part of the process is for Prodigal to remember the three keys to success over sin. First, admit it. Second, omit it. Third, forget it. Yes, you must forget your sin, but do not forget the pain you caused.

Since God is the expert at forgiveness, it is fitting to see how He deals with His memories. The Bible records in Hebrews 10:17, "And their sins and iniquities will I remember no more." His forgiveness precludes any impulse to remember our sins. How can an all-knowing God have a memory lapse? God's memory is not based upon His *ability* to remember but His *decision* not to remember our sins. God chooses what He will remember and chooses what He will forget. Thankfully, He has chosen to forget our sins. In fact, God *refuses* to remember our past sins under any circumstances!

How does God forget our sins? He forgets our sins because He has *forgiven* our sins. God operates on the same threefold promise with us as we should with others. God makes a choice to forgive, and, once done, He never throws up our past to us again. Not ever! By an act of His grace, He refuses to remember our sins of the past.

Next, God never tells anyone about the sins He has forgiven. Our past sins are no one's business. Our Heavenly Father does not air our dirty laundry to the world. He never discusses our past sins with us, and He certainly never discusses them with others. Micah 7:19 states that our past sins are "cast into the depths of the sea." Most everyone has heard by now the old statement that reminds us that God has put up a "No Fishing" sign to warn people to stay away from the sea where our sins are buried.

Finally, our magnificent and loving Lord never allows Himself to dwell on our past sins. He makes the choice not to allow them to cross His mind. God taught us that they were out of His sight; therefore, they are out of His mind. Since God never *thinks* about our past sins, He never *talks* about them, and since He never *talks* about them, He never *thinks* about them!

Has God ever been betrayed by us? Absolutely! Has He forgiven us? Absolutely! Has He removed our sins from His thoughts? Absolutely! Can we do the same with our transgressors if we follow His pattern? Absolutely!

The Apostle Paul teaches us how to handle our thoughts. We accomplish this by focusing on the roses instead of the thorns (Philippians 4:8). Prodigal, you and Betrayed may struggle with your memories for quite some time. The best way to win that battle is through the principle of displacement. Instead of trying to drive out the darkness, turn on a light. Instead of fixating on the *thorns* of your past sins or the pain of betrayal, focus on the *roses* of God's grace and mercy. Find a rose to concentrate on instead of allowing thorns to captivate your thoughts.

Paul tells the church that we should think about things that are "true, honest, just, pure, lovely, and of good report." Adultery does not fit into any one of these categories. Therefore, do not think about your past; think about your future. Prodigal, God wants you sin-free. Betrayed, God wants you pain-free. Try to envision your Heavenly Father running toward you to embrace you. Next comes the hugs and kisses. Then comes the celebration with a house full of friends. After that comes your very own fatted calf!

"Could someone please pinch me off a taste of that barbecue?" the prodigal is overheard to say.

I wrote the following lines just for you, my readers, who are struggling with the pain of sin, especially the sin of infidelity. It seems an appropriate perspective for both your natural and spiritual dimensions. Prodigals, I dedicate this to you and your spouses with my love and prayers as a reminder of God's love for you both.

"The Song of the Prodigal"
You met me with mercy,
You greeted me with grace,
You knew I had failed you and forfeited my place,
But with a robe, a ring, and your tender embrace,
You covered me in your love,
You met me with your mercy,
You greeted me with your grace.

redirection

"Is there life after divorce?"

This is the portion of the book I did not want to write. Some might refer to it as an e*pilogue*, while others might call it a *disclaimer*. Whatever you wish to call it, it is a stipulation to the fact that not all marriages survive the devastating effects of adultery. Therefore, we need to address those who will see the unavoidable dissolution of their marriage. What do they do?

The bombardment of questions resonates throughout the legal proceedings about what life will be like after the divorce is decreed. The future may seem like a blur of unresolved decisions that have to be made. Questions about housing, finances, division of property, custody of children, loneliness, and emptiness, coupled with the fearful prospects of future courtship, all swirl around in the mind as the inevitable approaches. Divorce *equals* death, or so it now seems.

For the Christian, this process of divorce is especially agonizing. After all, the church can be one of the most unforgiving places on earth. Many times the divorced are reduced to substandard membership. The asterisk is always associated with their name in the minds of other parishioners. Divorced individuals may be banished from the choir, the orchestra, the boardroom, the pulpit, or the pew.

We all know it is not fair, but we also know that it frequently happens. The pain of divorce is intensified by the false piety of the church, and the wounds just keep on coming. It does not happen at every church, but it is a practice far too common in the religious world. Moreover, to iterate an earlier statement, this reaction by the church is not right, but it is predictable.

Because of the rejection of the radically religious, many divorcees leave the church and flounder in a sea of disenfranchisement, disillusionment, disenchantment, and disgust. The place where they thought they would receive comfort, nurturing, healing, and understanding has, for all intents and purposes, shown them the "left foot of fellowship." Where does the divorced person turn now? To whom shall they go for love and healing of their broken heart? The answer is surprisingly simple: Go to Jesus!

Many think that Jesus and His church are synonymous. What a shock it is to discover that many of the churches that identify themselves with Christ are nothing like Him. Churches can be good, but Jesus is better. You will always find a welcome reception when you go to Him. Remember, He is the one who said in Matthew 11:28, "Come unto *me*, all ye that labor and are heavy laden, and I will give you rest" (emphasis mine). Jesus knew something about religious people, and that may be one reason why He suggested that you might need to bypass the religious institutions and come straight to Him when you are hurting.

Does Jesus offer a new lease on life for the divorced? Is there really a life for someone after their marriage is dissolved? The biblical answer is a resounding yes. That is the good news of the Gospel of Christ. However, let us look at the entire subject of divorce and remarriage from God's perspective. This will be a brief, but not reckless, look at divorce from His Word.

Divorce, by Old Testament definition, means "separation from bed and board." The New Testament word means "putting away," "cutting off, or dissolving" (Matthew 19:3, 6). The early church fathers struggled with their interpretation of Moses' writings on the subject of divorce (Deuteronomy 24). Hillel and Shammai, two leaders of the Jewish Rabbinical School at Jerusalem, saw it from opposite points of view. Hillel said you could divorce for "any or every cause," which supported the actions of the Jewish men whom Moses addressed. Meanwhile, Shammai's stricter interpretation of the Bible stated that divorce was restricted to only "one cause" (adultery).

Moses broached this subject because the Jewish men were divorcing their wives for burning the biscuits, being a poor housewife, or they simply met someone prettier. Moses had to tell the men that hastening to divorce was not acceptable with God. He never intended that people would be so careless with their marriage commitment. Remember, God created marriage; therefore, He reserves the right to establish the rules. Those early Jews were breaking the spirit, if not the laws, of the covenant of marriage. Forever since then, divorce and remarriage have been issues of gargantuan proportions for both society and the church.

Jesus actually rocked the ecclesiastical world with His conversation recorded in John 4. Upon meeting the woman at the well, He asked the whereabouts of her husband. She told Him that she had no husband. Then came the shot heard around the world, or at least throughout the church world. Jesus said, "You are correct. You *have* no husband! You *have had* five and the man you are presently living with is not your husband" (emphasis mine).

What was Jesus saying? He was stating that the laws regarding the disillusionment of marriage were so binding that, once divorced, it is as though you have never been married in God's eyes. His view is contrasted by the more popular concept that she *had* five husbands. The church calls them "living husbands or companions." Jesus taught that in God's sight *there is no living husband!* Jesus' words were both profound and radical, creating a shockwave of contradiction to the legalists of His day.

Moses spoke of former and latter husbands, but they were no longer husbands in the active, legal sense. Jesus taught the woman that cohabitation with a lover does not constitute marriage. So final was the divorce decree, or "Letter of Freedom," in the Bible that spouses were forbidden to return to their divorced companions. They could marry another person (Deuteronomy 24:1–2), but the divorce was as if there had never been a previous marriage. Do you see why Jesus invited us to come to Him? You will not find His theology of marriage expressed at very many of His places of worship.

Archbishop Trench of England once stated, "Failure to distinguish between word meanings is the Mother of all error." Because the church has not properly understood the finality of the biblical word "divorce," we have imposed limitations and exclusions upon the victims of divorce God never intended. Jesus' words to the woman at the well were not judgmental but emancipating. She was free to put her marriage failures behind her and discover the newness of life she had never known.

The common view on divorce in most of Christianity is to exercise extreme caution. This is exactly as it should be.

No one should demean or trivialize the vows of marriage. It is called "Holy Matrimony" for a reason. God established it as a parabolic view of His relationship with the church, the Bride of Christ. Please do not think that either Moses or I am an endorser of divorce. It is to be avoided if possible.

However, we also know that, unfortunately, divorce happens. We, the church of the Lord Jesus, are confronted with how we will react to the victims of divorce. If we use Christ's example in John 4, we will embrace the hurting with arms of love and acceptance. We do not have to condone the circumstances in order to compassionately minister to the person.

Jesus did not create a different kind of divorcement than that already given by Moses. He recognized that divorce meant permanent disillusionment of the marriage. Jesus' mission was to correct the abuses. He did not change it to a "separation bill," where the two are still tethered until eternity. Jesus actually reaffirmed the right to remarry as stated by Moses. Unlike under Moses, where adulterers were stoned, divorce was later mercifully substituted for stoning.

In Matthew 1:19, it states that Joseph, being a just man, was going to divorce Mary upon discovery of her pregnancy. He, no doubt, believed that divorce was more humane than stoning. In 1 Corinthians 7:15, Paul writes the church, giving permission from God for Christians to divorce a spouse on the grounds of *desertion*. Paul's view is much stricter than Hillel's and not quite as restrictive as Shammai's. Though Paul wrote to the early Church (1 Timothy 3) warning their leaders to be a *"one-woman kind of man"* and was very strong in his support of marriage, there was *never* any indication that Paul disdained or condemned any second marriages by these leaders.

Some of the greatest Greek scholars and sources down through history, like *Baker's Theological Dictionary*, Dr. A.T.

Robertson, Dr. Edersheim, Dr. Ramm, Dean Farrar, and Dr. Kenneth Weust, all conclude that Paul's warnings in Timothy were against polygamy, not divorce and remarriage. Their educated views are based upon translations, not interpretations, of the original texts of the Bible.

Leaders should definitely set the standard for the sanctity and monogamy of marriage. However, it is not seen anywhere in the Scriptures where God disqualifies someone on the basis of a divorce and subsequent remarriage, especially when the divorce was not of their initiation. Jesus certainly did not forbid the woman at the well from becoming the *first* evangelist in Samaria.

There is life indeed awaiting you after divorce. Jesus taught that adultery is *not a perpetual state* but a sin. He said to the woman caught in the act of adultery in John 8:11, "Neither do I condemn you, go and sin no more."

Many have asked what Jesus wrote in the sand when he was listening to her accusers. Here is another Frazierism: I suggest it could have been, "Where is the *man*? Remember, if she was caught 'in the act,' there had to be a partner there committing the act of adultery with her. What happened to him?

Adultery requires the presence of a man and a woman. Mosaic Law required that *both* of the participants be stoned. Why did these men not bring the man? Whatever Christ wrote, it was indicting enough that they 'dropped their stones and fled.'"

The Aramaic translation (the language Jesus primarily used) gives us this literal translation of the words of Christ in Matthew 19:9: "Whosoever marries her that is *shvikta* ("undivorced") does commit adultery." Jesus differentiates in the discourse between the Aramaic words "*shrita*" ("divorced, sacred bond is loosed") and the aforementioned "*shvikta*" ("undivorced, no papers served"). According to Lamsa's

Idioms In the Bible Explained, Jesus was condemning the laxity of the law where men grew tired of their wives and sent them away without divorcing them legally with the formal papers of divorcement. They basically deserted their wives, not divorced them.

Hebrews 11 tells us the harlot Rahab had her place of distinction in "Faith's Hall of Fame." Many other examples are in the Bible of God using imperfect people to carry His Gospel. He used murderers, liars, deceivers, thieves, adulterers, and felons of varying degrees to show forth the Glory of His salvation. Surely God can use you and me despite our past transgressions.

If your marriage is never restored, do not lose heart. God can redirect your life, and you will find that, through Jesus Christ and His precious blood, there is life after divorce. What is the quality of life that exists for the divorced person? It is the same life offered by Christ to the woman at the well. It is called in Greek "*Zoe.*"

Zoe is not a reference to biological existence or neurological functioning. In the Bible it literally refers to "life in an absolute sense, the life of God or life as the Father has it." This is a form of life that can only be realized through the indwelling of the Holy Spirit of God. It is the life of heaven, not the earth. It is celestial life, not terrestrial life.

Zoe is the same essence of life the Father and the Son possess. *Zoe* is the life of the Spirit, not the flesh. In John 10:10, Christ says, "The thief cometh not, but for to steal, and to kill, and to destroy: I am come that they might have *life*, and that they might have *it* more abundantly" (emphasis mine). He was referring to the *Zoe* life, not just a healthy respiratory system. Jesus proclaimed that there was an endless supply of the God-kind of life available to all *believers,* not just the perfect ones. His water satisfies the thirst of the heart when nothing else will.

Is this "God-life" available to the divorced? Absolutely! Will Christ allow His life (*zoe*) to reside in you and flow out from you to minister to others? Absolutely! According to Christ's own words of ministry in John 4:14 to the woman at the well of Sychar with quintuple divorces on her courthouse record, "Whosoever drinketh of the water that I shall give him shall never thirst; but the water that I shall give him shall be in him a well of water springing up into everlasting 'life'" (Greek *zoe*).

Feeling as though you are a failure at marriage does not doom you to being a failure at faith. The only qualification Christ gives for receiving His "God-kind of life" is not whether you are divorced, it is whether you are thirsty. Be encouraged and drink heartily. There is eternal life for *you* after divorce.

invitation

There is no one better suited to help you navigate through life than the Lord Jesus Christ. If you have never accepted Him as the Savior and Lord of your life, you are missing one of the greatest opportunities to find help, hope, and healing for your troubled soul.

A simple heartfelt prayer is all it takes to invite Him into your life as your Savior. He will respond by giving you His free gift of eternal salvation from your sin. That is why the Lord Jesus came to earth, suffered, and died and was resurrected from the grave. Jesus Christ will pardon you and give you His abiding peace. Why not do that right now? You will never regret your decision.

If you, as a Christian or a new convert, would like some free literature to help you in your walk with Christ, contact our office through our Web site: www.donfrazier.com

resources

The following is a list of resources that have been especially helpful in the development of this book, either by direct quotation or by summation and paraphrasing.

Adams, Jay E. Competent to Counsel. Baker Book House.

Adams, Jay E. The Christian Counselor's Manual. Baker Book House.

Divry's Modern English-Greek and Greek-English Desk Dictionary, D.C. Divry, Inc., Publishers.

The American Heritage Dictionary of the English Language, Fourth Edition. 2006. Houghton Mifflin Company.

Analytical Greek New Testament. Baker Book House.

Betcher, Dr. William. Seven Basic Quarrels in Marriage. Villard Books.

The Complete Word Study Dictionary of the New Testament. AMG Publishers.

Earle, Ralph. Word Meanings in the New Testament. Hendrickson Publishers.

Kernerman English Multilingual Dictionary (Beta Version). 2000–2006. K Dictionaries Ltd.

George M. Lamsa. Idioms in the Bible Explained and A Key to the Original Gospels. Harper and Row Publishers.

Merriam-Webster's Collegiate Dictionary Eleventh Edition. 2004.

The Nestle Greek Text of the New Testament.

The New Linguistic and Exegetical Key to the Greek New Testament. Zondervan.

The New Living Translation. Tyndale House Publishers.

The New Strong's Complete Concordance. Thomas Nelson Publishers.

Online Etymology Dictionary. 2001. Douglas Harper.

Random House Unabridged Dictionary. 2006. Random House, Inc.

Robertson, A.T. A Grammar of the Greek New Testament. Broadman Press.

The Septuagint. Hendrickson Publishers.

Vine's Expository Dictionary of New Testament Words. Fleming H. Revell Publisher.

Wuest, Kenneth. The New Testament, An Expanded Translation. Eerdmans Publishing Company.

about the author

His piano artistry has blessed and inspired people of all ages...his insightful presentation of the Word of God has elevated many listeners to a greater level of Christian living...his compassion for the hurting has resulted in many being healed from both physical and emotional disorders.

As an ordained minister, Dr. Donald M. Frazier has witnessed a special calling and anointing from God upon his life. Listed below are a few of the highlights from his more than forty-four years of continuous service to the Lord Jesus Christ.

- Traveled with professional gospel quartet serving as their manager and pianist
- Recording artist with six singing and piano albums to his credit
- Fulltime representative for the International Youth Department of denomination
- Served as West Coast representative for Department of Publications of denomination
- Traveled as an evangelist for over sixteen years

- Served in State and local denominational positions of leadership
- Over eighteen years of successful pastoral ministry
- Respected Marriage and Family Specialist with fourteen seminars taught at Heritage USA
- Graduate of the Criminal Justice Academy of South Carolina
- Adjunct Chaplain and Counselor at Colorado State Penitentiary
- Served as uniformed Police Chaplain and Counseling Consultant for two municipalities
- After receiving Ph.D. degree, opened Faith Clinic Counseling Center offering Christ-centered psychological & spiritual counseling
- Frequent TV appearances, including PTL, TBN, and Daystar telecasts
- Hosted Atonement Ministries' nationally syndicated TV program "Adventures In Faith"
- Founder and President of Atonement Ministries, Inc., an evangelistic, missionary, and media ministry reaching around the world with the Gospel of Jesus Christ.

Dr. Frazier's services include uplifting, Christ-exalting music coupled with exciting ministry from the Word and a special anointing for ministering *help, hope, & healing* through the work of the Holy Spirit. He and his wife, Abbie, reside in the Houston, Texas area. He is also author of *Greek Nuggets from the Gospel Gold Mine.*